The Book of Devi

IN THE SAME SERIES

The Book of Devi by Bulbul Sharma

The Book of Vishnu by Nanditha Krishna

The Book of Shiva by Namita Gokhale

The Book of Krishna by Pavan K. Varma

The Book of Ganesha by Royina Grewal

FORTHCOMING IN THE SERIES

The Book of Brahma by Renuka Narayanan

The Book of Hanuman by Parvez Dewan

The Book of Saraswati by Namita Gokhale

The Book of Lakshmi by Bulbul Sharma

ALSO AVAILABLE FROM PENGUIN

The Hanuman Chalisa of Goswami Tulasi Das
translated by Parvez Dewan

Rehras: Evensong—The Sikh Evening Prayer translated
by Reema Anand and Khushwant Singh

The Name of My Beloved: Verses of the Sikh Gurus
translated by Nikky Guninder Kaur Singh

The Book of Prayer compiled and edited by Renuka
Narayanan

The Book of
Devi

BULBUL SHARMA

PENGUIN
VIKING

VIKING

Penguin Books India (P) Ltd., 11 Community Centre, Panchsheel Park, New Delhi 110 017, India
Penguin Books Ltd., 80 Strand, London WC2R 0RL, UK
Penguin Group Inc., 375 Hudson Street, New York, NY 10014, USA
Penguin Books Australia Ltd., 250 Camberwell Road, Camberwell, Victoria 3124, Australia
Penguin Books Canada Ltd., 10 Alcorn Avenue, Suite 300, Toronto, Ontario, M4V 3B2, Canada
Penguin Books (NZ) Ltd., Cnr Rosedale & Airborne Roads, Albany, Auckland, New Zealand
Penguin Books (South Africa) (Pty) Ltd., 24 Sturdee Avenue, Rosebank 2196, South Africa

First published in Viking by Penguin Books India 2001

Text copyright © Bulbul Sharma 2001

Illustrations copyright © Penguin Books India 2001

10 9 8 7 6 5

Illustrations by Amitabh

Typeset in Sabon by Mantra Virtual Services
Printed at Saurabh Printers Pvt. Ltd., Noida

For Ma

Acknowledgement is made to Sri Ramakrishna Math, Mylapore, Chennai, India, for permission to reprint 'Hymn to Aparajita' from Devimahatmyam.

Contents

Introduction   1

Durga   9

Sati   31

Lakshmi   45

Saraswati   61

Sita   77

Radha   107

Ganga   129

Village Goddesses and Minor Deities   143

Hymn to Aparajita   158

Bibliography   162

Contents

Introduction

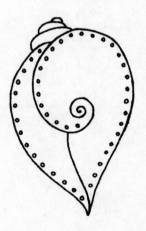

My search for the Devi began when I was six years old. My grandmother's chanting would wake me up at dawn and I would crawl out of the mosquito net, walking blindly towards the sound of that faint voice. The pooja room was always lit up by an ancient bedside lamp which cast a rosy glow on the faces of the deities. Everyone was here. A gleaming, bejewelled Kali carved out of granite, a pristine white Shiva, a fiery-eyed Durga, a baby Krishna asleep in his cradle and various other gods and goddesses whom my grandmother wanted to please with her prayers. The pooja room with its collection of tiny silver plates and glasses, miniature beds and lace pillows, sparkling at dawn with jasmine buds which had just been plucked, fascinated me as a child. I would sit outside at the door, since I had not yet bathed, and watch her movements as she did aarti and laid out the bhog. The fragrance of incense would make my head swim and I would inch closer to the marble statue of Radha, hoping my grandmother would give the first prasad to me.

Later as an adult when I began to be interested in mythology, those images lit by the first rays of dawn would repeatedly appear in front of my eyes: Kali's flashing eyes above the delicate nose glittering with a diamond nose-ring, Durga's red silk saree with a thin border of gold, Krishna's plump little hands curled into a fist. They would come into my thoughts not like deities but like living people, with likes and dislikes, complaining of hunger, fatigue and boredom and sharing their everyday joys. I regret not paying more attention to what my grandmother was chanting, not remembering each word of the stories she told me at night. 'Then came Durga with her four children. Kartika was crying and Ganesha was hungry as usual. Lakshmi sat quietly but Saraswati was grumbling away angrily. What could Ma do? Shiva had, once again, not brought anything to eat today,' she would say as if it had happened just yesterday and these were not words from a mythical legend centuries old.

Maybe if I had listened more carefully, I would now understand the Devi more. I would not be so confused about the goddess as she changes her forms, the colour of her skin, the expression of her eyes. Uma, Durga, Parvati, Lakshmi and Saraswati, are they one or are they different? When do they separate and when do they merge? Is Saraswati Vishnu's wife or Brahma's consort? When does Durga change into Kali?

If I had listened more carefully, I would have known from childhood the Devi's 1008 names which my grandmother chanted effortlessly each morning, in between giving instructions to the cook. As I read the Devi Bhagavata Purana, make notes from the Devimahatmyam, search for the real Radha and Sita in the epics, I wish I could go back in time to that dimly lit pooja room and listen once more to the chanting. Then I would know why Durga is also called Katyayani; how she turned into Kaushiki in just a fleeting moment; how she slayed the demon Mahishasura. Why was Shiva not invited to Daksha's great sacrifice? Why did Saraswati leave Vaikunth? These myths were retold over and over again as my grandmother chanted her prayers and sang to herself in that lonely hour of the morning. Her voice was jagged with age and sometimes she just hummed to herself, reciting the verses in her mind, or she would place her spectacles on the tip of her nose and read aloud from a heavy red cloth-bound book. Now, after four decades, I know it was the Bhagavata Purana, a treasure trove of mythological stories.

The two great epics, the *Ramayana* and the *Mahabharata* and the Puranas have been the source of most of the stories in this collection though I have included some popular folk myths too which are not found in the Puranas. The main Puranas like the Devi Bhagavata Purana sing the praises of the particular god but they also contain stories associated with other gods and goddesses. Many of the legends, like Sati's sacrifice, are repeated in many of the Puranas but each one has a different ending to it. The lead role is always played by the god in whose praise the Purana has been compiled, while the other gods and goddesses are given minor parts to play. A detailed account of planets, sacred rivers and trees, divine birds and animals associated with the god is also given in the Puranas. The Devi Bhagavata Purana deals mostly with Durga's powerful image but we meet many other goddesses in the legends. Are they one or are they different? Are they different manifestations of the same goddess? Has their original Vedic image been confused by the later Puranas which abound in extravagant imagery much more suited to popular literature?

The goddesses mentioned in Vedic literature were never as powerful as the gods. For instance Usha, a popular goddess who has been mentioned repeatedly in the Vedas and has many hymns addressed to her, still does not rank as a superior deity. Many of the goddesses like Usha, Aditi and Prithvi from Vedic literature did not survive or were reduced in stature by the time the Puranas were compiled. Saraswati is one of the few goddesses who is mentioned in both Vedic and Puranic traditions as the goddess of learning and wisdom and retains that position even today. Important goddesses like Parvati, Durga, Kali, Radha and Sita are not mentioned in early Vedic literature though they assumed powerful forms later and are worshipped in various temples and other sacred places all over India today.

Durga is the most popular goddess in Bengal and is worshipped annually with great fanfare, while in the north there are shrines in almost every village dedicated to Parvati. Lakshmi reigns in the south as a benevolent goddess and Radha and Sita have a comparatively small but devoted band of followers. Popular tales about these goddesses are recited almost daily in many households, and children get to know them from an early age. Which child would not be fascinated by the wonderful imagery? Fiery-eyed Durga astride a golden lion; Saraswati resplendent in white along with her swan; a glowing Lakshmi seated on a lotus in bloom; and Kali with her frightening garland of skulls. The legends that surround them are told over and over again and soon the children know them by heart. For them, as it is for me, these beautiful lotus-eyed goddesses are not just religious icons but part of one's family. They laugh and cry, quarrel with each other over petty things, they have fragile natures despite their powerful forms. They are often jealous, angry, greedy and plot deviously against their enemies but still they need to be loved by their devotees. Then they appear, splendid, glorious and benevolent, to dazzle us with their all-pervading light.

Durga

Durga, the great goddess with a thousand names and innumerable forms, appears as Shiva's consort in many legends, intensifying his attributes. But she is also, unlike most other goddesses of Hindu mythology, worshipped as an embodiment of female energy. She is the formidable Devi and Mahadevi and has many other powerful independent female forms. In a hymn recited by Arjuna in the *Mahabharata*, her many names are mentioned, '. . . Reverence be to thee, Siddha-Senani, the noble, the dweller of Mandara, Kumari, Kali, Kapali, Kapila, Krishnapingala. Reverence to thee, Bhadrakali; reverence to thee, Maha Kali, Chandi, Chanda, Tarini, Varavarini. O fortunate Kalyayani, O Karali, O Vijaya, O Jaya, younger sister of the chief of cowherds [Krishna], delighting always in Mahisha's blood! O Uma, Sakambhari, thou art white one, thou black one! O destroyer of Kaitabha! O sciences, thou art the science of Brahma, the great sleep of embodied beings. O mother of Skanda [Kartika], divine Durga, dweller in wilderness! Thou, great goddess, art praised with a pure heart. By thy favour let me ever be victorious in battle.'

There are several accounts of Durga's origin in the various Puranas. In the Vishnu Purana she arises from Vishnu as his magical force. He calls upon her to help delude a demon king who is threatening to kill the baby Krishna. She takes Krishna's place in Devaki's womb, saving him and allowing herself to be killed by the demon. Krishna, an incarnation of Vishnu, promises her that in doing so she would become 'assimilated to him in glory; she would obtain an eternal place in the sky; be installed by Indra amongst the gods; obtain a perpetual abode on the Vindhya mountains, where meditating upon him (Vishnu) she would kill two demons, Sumbha and Nisumbha, and would be worshipped with animal sacrifices'.

Durga is still represented, as she was centuries ago, as a golden-faced woman of great beauty with ten arms. In her right hand she holds a spear with which she is piercing the demon Mahisha. In her other hands she holds an array of formidable weapons. A lion, her mount, leans against her, its golden mane a contrast to her blood-red saree.

Idols of Durga in Bengal, where she is the reigning deity, depict the goddess with her four children: Lakshmi, Saraswati, Kartika and Ganesha. A small image of Shiva, her consort, is painted above her head. Durga Pooja, an important festival of Bengal and other parts of northern India, is celebrated for nine days in autumn. The central image of Durga slaying the demon Mahisha is installed on the first day and verses from the Devimahatmyam are recited during these nine days. Buffalo and goat sacrifices were once a part of the celebration though now a pumpkin is cut as a ceremonial offering. Devotees sing, dance and feast, watched by the benevolent goddess and her family. Popular legends believe she is on a brief visit from her abode in the Himalayas where she lives with Shiva. On the last day of the Durga Pooja, the idol is immersed in the nearest river with a great fanfare of music and dancing to bid the goddess farewell till she returns again the next autumn.

Though Durga Pooja is celebrated in autumn, in some parts of rural Bengal she is also worshipped during spring. The reason for this is found in a legend from the Kalika Purana and Devi Bhagavata Purana, though Valmiki's *Ramayana* does not mention it.

Ravana, the king of Lanka, was a great devotee of Durga and worshipped her according to strict rituals every spring. Rama was advised by Narada to invoke the goddess since only she could help him win this battle. 'Time and again the mighty goddess has come to help the righteous. All the gods in heaven pray to her when they want to defeat their foes. You too shall win this battle and regain Sita, who this evil Ravana has abducted, if you gain the favour of the goddess by worshipping her according to the method that is proper,' said Narada to Rama. The prince of Ayodhya then performed the pooja in autumn since he could not wait for spring. The goddess transferred her favour from Ravana to Rama, helping him win the battle.

While instructing Rama on how the goddess should be worshipped, Narada tells him that the goddess was worshipped by the gods Indra, Shiva and Vishnu when they needed her help to defeat their enemies.

In later centuries too Durga was associated with military success and came to be worshipped by kings before a battle. Shivaji, the great Maratha ruler, is said to have received his sword from Bhavani herself. The founder ruler of Mewar, Bappa, according to a folk legend, received his sword from the goddess. After he had spent many days without food and water, wandering in the forest, the goddess Durga suddenly appeared before him on her golden lion and gave him a lance, a bow, a quiver full of arrows, a shield and a sword—a sword made in heaven by Vishwakarma himself.

The Markandaya Purana lists Durga's 1008 names. Many of these names are derived from the form she assumes to battle with various demons to save the gods. According to the Skanda Purana the Devi was named Durga because she slew a demon named Durga.

The Devimahatmyam, or the Greatness of Devi, forms a part of the Markandaya Purana. A poem of 700 verses, it is one of the main sources for the mythology of the Mahadevi. This sacred textbook for worshippers of Devi in her forms as Durga, Parvati, Uma and Kali is recited in her temples and is known as the Chandipath. The following prayer is invoked during ceremonies devoted to the Devi:

I resort to Mahalakshmi, the destroyer of Mahishasura, who is seated on the lotus, is of the complexion of coral and who holds in her (eighteen) hands rosary, axe, mace, arrow, thunderbolt, lotus, bow, pitcher, rod, sakti, sword, shield, conch, bell, wine-cup, trident, noose, and the discus Sudarshana.

In this legend from the Devimahatmyam, the goddess, created by the light of three gods—Brahma, Vishnu and Shiva, assumes her most powerful form to slay the buffalo-demon Mahishasura and is thus called, thereafter, Mahishasuramardini.

A war between the asuras and the devas had been on for a hundred years and finally the king of asuras, Mahishasura, defeated Indra and became the lord of heaven. Victorious and full of pride, the king of asuras now assumed the powers of all the devas. He was not only Indra, but Surya, Agni, Chandra, Yama and Varuna. The vanquished devas wandered for a while like helpless mortals and then weary and tired they finally reached Vaikunth to take shelter with Lord Vishnu. 'See our plight, O lord. The mighty Indra is without his heaven, Surya has no light, Agni has turned as cold as water and Vayu too is still. Look how faded Chandra has become and Yama and Varuna stand before you as helpless as mortal men. Help us, O lord. Destroy this evil Mahishasura who has reduced us to this.'

When Vishnu saw his devas reduced to this sorry state and heard their voices full of sorrow, he was filled with anger. His face trembled and a fierce light shot from his eyes, straight as a lance. Shiva too appeared, enraged, with a great light, and then Brahma came and joined them, his face on fire with intense anger. From the bodies of all the other devas arrows of powerful light and energy shot forth. This combined concentration of light rose like a blazing mountain, its flames lighting up all the three worlds with a unique golden light. And then as the circle of devas watched, the light slowly gathered itself into a lustrous female form.

By that which was Shiva's light her face came into being, by Yama's her hair, by Vishnu's her arms, and by Chandra's her breasts. By Indra's her waist, by Varuna's her thighs, and by earth's light her hips. By Brahma's light her feet came into being, by Surya's her toes, by Agni's her three eyes were formed and the light of Vayu became her ears. The lights of all other devas too surged forward and they were filled with joy as they beheld the auspicious and beautiful Devi who had been thus formed.

Then Shiva reached for his trident and from it he formed a new trident which he gave to the Devi. Vishnu gave her a discus made from his own discus and Varuna gave her a conch. Agni gave the newly formed goddess a spear, and Indra, the lord of devas, brought out a thunderbolt from his own thunderbolt and presented it to her. Yama gave her a staff from his own staff of death, and Varuna, the lord of waters, gave her a noose. Brahma, the lord of beings, gave her a string of beads and a water-pot, and Surya bestowed his own golden rays on her skin so that the goddess shimmered in her own light. Jewels for her crest, necklaces, earrings, anklets and bracelets were given to her by the devas. Vishwakarma gave her a shining axe and the ocean brought for her garlands of everlasting lotuses. The mountain Himavat gave the Devi a mighty lion to ride on. Glittering with jewels from the milk-ocean, armed with an array of celestial weapons, shining with a divine light, the Devi gave a roar of laughter. As she laughed, stepping out from within the circle of devas, her mighty voice filled the entire sky. She laughed again and again making all the three worlds tremble. The mountains rocked and the seas churned with her terrible laughter. 'Victory to you!' cried all the devas in joy and the sages bowed their heads as she walked.

Mahishasura heard the Devi's footsteps which made the earth quake and looked up to see who was making all this commotion. 'I am the lord of this universe now. The sky, the earth and the oceans lie crushed beneath my feet. Who dares to make this terrible noise in my presence?' he said angrily and rushed towards the roar that was filling the sky and the seas. Then he saw her.

The Devi stood pervading the three worlds with her lustre. The earth lay curved and bent under her footstep, her glittering diadem scraped the sky.

Then began a battle between the Devi and Mahishasura. The sky blazed as weapons were hurled by the mighty army of asuras. Hundreds of thousands of elephant soldiers, millions of foot soldiers, cavalry and ten million charioteers fought in this great battle. One by one, great asuras surrounded by thousands of crores of elephants, chariots and horses were sent by Mahishasura to battle with the Devi. They rushed at her with iron maces, javelins and spears. With clubs, swords and axes they tried to kill her. The Devi sat regal and still on her lion, bathed in her circle of unique light. The weapons the asuras hurled at her could not touch her, and she rode her lion through the battlefield, cutting them effortlessly. The lion's mane shook with rage as they stalked the army of asuras like a fire raging through a forest. While she fought, the goddess played on a battle drum and blew her conch to announce the victory which would soon be hers. Every time she heaved a sigh during the battle it would turn into a battalion of thousand men. The Devi killed hundreds of asuras with her trident, club, showers of spears, swords and stunned thousands of asuras by the noise of her bell and conch. Her swift arrows flew across the battlefield, piercing the asuras till they began to look like porcupines. Some had their heads cut off by her lightning sword while the others were torn into pieces by her axe. The battlefield was soon turned into a mountain of dead asuras, elephants, horses and chariots that had been felled by her. A river of blood flooded the earth as the Devi destroyed the vast army in no time. The generals of the army of asuras, astounded at how their mighty army was being routed, came forward to battle with the Devi, but they too were killed by her.

Then as his army and his generals were being destroyed, Mahishasura raged with terrible anger and assumed his buffalo form. He stormed into the battlefield killing everyone in his way with a blow of his muzzle. His hooves stamped the Devi's army to death and those who managed to escape were pierced by his mighty horns. Very soon Mahishasura had laid low the Devi's army and charged towards her lion. Pounding the earth with his hooves, Mahishasura raged ahead, tossing the high mountains with his horns as his terrible bellowing filled the sky. The earth began to disintegrate under his weight and, lashed by his tail, the seas overflowed. Pierced by his horns the clouds broke into fragments and mountains trembled and collapsed on the earth.

When the Devi saw Mahishasura charging towards her she called all the powers that the devas had given her and assumed her most terrible form. Now raged a battle between the two of them which was so frightening in its intensity that even the devas looking down from the skies shut their eyes. As swift as wind, Durga threw her noose over the buffalo demon's head, but as soon as he was bound Mahishasura quit his buffalo form and became a lion. Then as soon as the Devi cut off his head he made himself a man with a sword. The Devi with lightning speed cut off his head but Mahishasura became a giant elephant. With his huge trunk, the elephant attacked the Devi's lion but as he was dragging him away, she beheaded him with her sword. Then once more, Mahishasura resumed his buffalo form and began to shake the three worlds with his rage. The Devi too was filled with fury and her eyes turned red with anger. She gave a great leap filling the sky, landed on the asura pressing his neck down with her foot and impaled him with her spear. Giving a great howl of pain Mahishasura became half asura and half buffalo as he fought to free himself. The goddess lifted her great sword and with one mighty blow cut off his head. As soon as he was killed, Mahishasura's entire army of asuras too perished with a collective sigh.

The host of devas and all the sages bowed before the Devi as the gandharvas sang and the apsaras danced. One by one, the devas came forward to sing their words of gratitude and to praise the victorious goddess. They worshipped her with flowers from the divine garden Nandan, anointed her with sacred unguents and lit incense.

'O Devi, we bow before you, who are yourself good fortune in the dwellings of the virtuous and ill-fortune in those of the vicious; intelligence in the hearts of the learned; faith in the hearts of the good; and modesty in the hearts of the high-born. May you protect the universe.'

The Devi is called upon again and again to save the devas from the asuras. In this legend from Devimahatmyam, goddess Parvati, the consort of Shiva, assumes the form of Chandika—a goddess who emerges from her own body—to kill two asuras, Sumbha and Nisumbha. Various names are given to the Devi as she battles with the demons and the famous hymn to Aparajita, or hymn to the unvanquished, forms a part of this poem.

'I meditate on the incomparable Mahasaraswati who holds in her lotus-like hands bell, trident, plough, conch, mace, bow and arrow; who is radiant like the moon shining at the fringe of a cloud; who is the destroyer of Sumbha and other asuras; who issued forth from Parvati's body.'

Sumbha and Nisumbha were two giant asuras who right from childhood wanted to be rulers of the three worlds. They decided to do many years of severe penance and even though they were young boys they set out with a firm resolution on their ambitious path. For ten thousand years they sat without food or water till Shiva finally appeared and granted them a boon that their strength and wealth would be greater than that of the devas. As soon as this was said, the two brothers declared war upon Indra's kingdom. Bold and arrogant with their new-found powers, the two asuras soon reduced the devas to slaves. They took over all the sacrifices made to the various devas who quietly went away from heaven and began to live as beggars on earth.

After surviving for a while in this wretched state, they remembered the promise the Devi had made to them. 'She had granted us the boon: "Whenever in calamites you think of me, that very moment I will put an end to all your miseries."' Gathering together their feeble remaining strength they made their way back to heaven and began to pray to Devi.

'Salutation to the Devi, to the Mahadevi. Salutation always to her who is ever auspicious. Salutation to her who is the primordial cause and embodiment of all that is good and benign. To thee we offer our humble obeisance,' sang the devas. As they sat on the banks of the river Ganga praying, Parvati came to bathe in the river. She listened for a while to the songs of prayer and then asked, 'Who is praised by you here?' As she said these words a goddess sprang from her and replied, 'This hymn is addressed to me by the assembled devas who have been vanquished by the two asuras Sumbha and Nisumbha.' The goddess who had emerged from Parvati shone before the devas, assuring them of victory over the asuras. Then she went away to the Himalayas where she began to live in a splendid garden she created.

One day Chanda and Munda, two powerful asuras who served the asura king Sumbha, saw the beautiful goddess alone in the forest. They were astounded by her beauty and raced back to their king to tell him about her. 'O King, a certain woman, most unsurpassingly beautiful, dwells there shedding lustre on Mount Himalaya. Such supreme beauty was never seen by anyone anywhere. Ascertain who that goddess is and take possession of her, O lord of the asuras.' By then Sumbha had captured all the precious jewels in the world. Airavata, the gem among elephants, was his after he stole it from Indra along with the heavenly Parijata tree. Brahma's chariot yoked with swans was also his now and so was the gold-showering umbrella of Varuna. The rare horse Uchchaishravas which emerged during the churning of the milk-ocean too was his. Sumbha, who possessed all this wealth, now wondered why this jewel of a woman was not his. He sent a messenger, Sugriva, to the Devi asking her to quickly come to him. Sugriva found the Devi in a garden on a mountain peak and gave her the message Sumbha had sent. 'O beautiful lady, whatever other rare objects there existed among the devas, gandharvas and nagas are with me.

'We look upon you, O Devi, as the jewel of womankind in the world. Come to me, since we are amongst those who enjoy the best objects.

'Wealth, great beyond compare, you will get by marrying me. Think over this in your mind and become my life.'

The Devi heard the messenger patiently and then she said in a gentle voice, 'You have spoken the truth. Sumbha is indeed the lord of the three worlds and so is Nisumbha. But I made a foolish promise to myself in my youth that I will only marry he who conquers me in battle. I shall only take for my husband the man who removes my pride and is my match in strength. So let the great Sumbha or Nisumbha defeat me here and take my hand in marriage.'

The messenger was aghast. How dare she, a mere woman, challenge his master, the king of the three worlds? He rushed back to relate her words to Sumbha. The king of asuras roared with anger and ordered his general Dhumralochana to go at once and fetch the proud Devi by force. 'Drag that shrew by her hair. Slay anyone who stands up as her saviour be it a god, yaksha or gandharva,' he thundered. Accompanied by sixty thousand asuras, the general rushed to the mountain peak where the Devi stood. 'Come to my lord, proud woman. If you do not then I will drag you there by your hair.' The Devi stood still and smiled. 'You have been sent by the lord of asuras. You are so mighty yourself with this vast army. What can I do if you take me by force?' she said. Dhumralochana rushed towards her and as he approached her, the Devi uttered a contemptuous sigh of 'hum' reducing the giant asura to a pile of ashes. When Sumbha heard this news, trembling with rage, he commanded his two chief generals to go and fetch the Devi. 'Bind her, let the asuras strike her, wound her. And then bring that shrew here at once,' he roared.

Chanda and Munda marched towards the mountains with a vast army. They saw the Devi on a golden peak seated upon her lion smiling gently. The asuras charged at her with their bows arched and shining swords. The Devi saw them coming towards her and suddenly her skin turned dark with rage. Out of her forehead, fierce and dark with a frowning brow, there suddenly emerged Kali. The terrible goddess glowing with rage was armed with a noose and a gleaming sword. In her hand she held a skull-topped staff decorated with a garland of skulls and from her gaping mouth her tongue lolled out. Crying out with a bloodthirsty roar which filled the sky, the furious goddess began to devour the asuras. Chanda and Munda rushed forward to engage her in battle, but before they could do so, the dark goddess mounted her lion, seized Chanda by his hair and cut his head off with her sword. Then she struck at Munda severing his head in one stroke. 'From now on you shall be called Chamunda for you have destroyed Chanda and Munda so fearlessly,' said the Devi.

Sumbha, raging with fury, now prepared to go into battle himself along with an army of a hundred crore giant asuras. When the gods saw this sea of asuras snaking towards the mountains they knew they had to help the goddess in her encounter with Sumbha and Nisumbha. So out of each of their bodies emerged a 'shakti' goddess endowed with the same strength and power. From Brahma came Brahmani, riding a chariot drawn by swans. She carried a rosary and a kamandal of water which she would sprinkle to make the asuras inert. From Shiva came Maheshvari adorned with a digit of the moon and garland of snakes. She was seated on a bull and held a shimmering trident in her hand. The shakti of Vishnu, Vaishnavi, came riding on the celestial bird holding a conch, discus, sword and bow in her hands. Many other gods too sent their shaktis to the battlefield and each of these was armed with a formidable weapon.

Then Devi Chandika sent a final warning to the king of asuras. Since she chose Shiva to be her ambassador she became known from then on as Shiva-duti. 'Tell the two arrogant asuras to go and live in the nether world and let the devas rule again. If through pride they are anxious to battle, come on then. Let my jackals be satiated with their flesh.'

The king of asuras heard this challenge and stormed ahead, mad with rage. He hurled arrows, spears, javelins and axes at her. The Devi calmly faced him with a full-drawn bow. Then with a light touch she let fly a huge arrow which shot all his weapons to pieces. Kali pierced the enemies with her spear, Brahmani sprinkled water which left them bereft of valour, an angry Maheshvari slew the asuras with her trident and Vaishnavi threw her discus, cutting them into pieces. The other shaktis too created havoc.

When the great asura Raktabija saw his army being vanquished by these enraged shaktis sent by the gods, he strode forward to join the battle. This asura had a boon that whenever a drop of blood fell from his body on the ground, an asura of his stature would rise from that very spot. As they fought, blood flowed from his body and a whole new army of asuras rose up at once to battle the Devi and the shaktis. Soon the entire world was filled with giant asuras and the devas were filled with alarm. Seeing the devas dejected Chandika laughed and said to Kali, 'O Chamunda open your mouth wide and drink this blood that flows from the asura.' So as the Devi showered the giant with arrows, spears and darts, Chamunda went on drinking his blood without letting a drop fall on the ground.

Sumbha, enraged on seeing his great army slaughtered, rushed to slay Chandika. Then began a battle between Sumbha and Nisumbha and the great Devi. Thunderbolts struck like arrows of fire and the sky was filled with war cries as they roared. Nisumbha tried to strike the Devi's lion with his sword but she quickly cut him into pieces. When Nisumbha fell, Sumbha came out on his chariot, holding an array of weapons in his eight arms. The goddess now blew her conch and began pulling at her bow string to make a deafening sound. Her lion roared too as the Devi enlarging her palms struck the sky with a ominous shrill cry of laughter. 'Victory to thee, O Devi!' cried the devas as they watched the terrible battle. The three worlds shook with their war cries as Devi split the arrows shot by Sumbha and he too retaliated by cutting her arrows down. Brahmani, Maheshvari, Vaishnavi and the other shaktis too jumped into the battlefield once more to slay the asuras. With his brother slain and his army slaughtered, Sumbha's rage knew no bounds. 'O Durga,' he shouted with anger, 'You who are so puffed up with pride, you are so haughty yet you resort to help from others when you fight.' When the Devi heard his voice she stood still and faced him. 'I am all alone in the world here. Who else is there beside me? See, O vile one, these goddesses, who are but my own powers, entering into my ownself.' Then one by one all the shaktis were absorbed in the body of the Devi. 'The numerous forms which I projected by my power here have been withdrawn by me, and now I stand alone. Now ready yourself for the final battle.'

Then, as the devas watched, began a terrible battle which lasted for a long time. Sumbha brought out all the divine weapons in his possession but the Devi destroyed them all. After carrying on a fierce fight which rose like a whirlwind of fury into the sky, the Devi lifted him up, whirled him around and flung him down. Then she plunged her spear into his heart and he fell lifeless on the ground, shaking the entire earth and flooding the seas. As soon as the evil asura was slain the universe became calm and peaceful. The sky became clear once more and the dark storm clouds turned tranquil. The rivers kept within their course and as the devas rejoiced, the sun became brilliant, the sacred fires burnt peacefully. A soothing calm now pervaded the world which had been so rocked by battlecries and the gandharvas sang in praise of the Devi:

'O Devi, be pleased and protect us always from fear of foes, as you have done just now by the slaughter of asuras. And destroy quickly the sins of all worlds and the great calamities which have sprung from evil portents.'

Sati

As Sati, a manifestation of Durga, the goddess is the beloved wife of Shiva. We see her now not as a great warrior but as his faithful, gentle wife Uma, who cannot bear the humiliation of her husband, whom she worships as a god, and gives up her life. Her name Sati has come to mean virtuous and it also describes a wife who commits self-immolation on her husband's funeral pyre. The following legend is from the Bhagavata Purana and there are various other versions of this legend in the *Mahabharata* and Skanda Purana.

One day Uma was sitting with her husband, Lord Shiva, in their home on Mount Kailash when she saw a convoy of glittering chariots passing by. Each one carried a finely bedecked god and his consort. They passed by in a flurry of golden dust and Uma, curious to know what was happening, stood up to gaze at this magnificent convoy. 'Where are they all going? All these gods and goddesses and even the gandharvas. Look, my lord, how they are all dressed up in fine clothes and jewels. You who knows all must know where they are going, dressed in their finest clothes and jewels?' she asked Shiva who was sitting quietly by her side. At first the great lord was silent, but when Uma asked him over and over again, he told her with great reluctance, 'They are all going to your father's house to take part in a great sacrifice he has organized.'

'But why have we, my lord, not been invited?' she

asked, bewildered. Shiva did not answer her though he knew why they had not been invited. The great god Rudra was silent because he knew his answer would hurt Uma. His father-in-law, Daksha, who was Brahma's son, had always disliked him and had been against his marrying his beautiful daughter Uma. 'My virtuous fawn-eyed daughter's hand to be given in marriage to this monkey-eyed god? A man who lives amongst the dead, wears bark and adorns himself with ash?' he had protested. But Brahma had told him to let Uma marry Shiva.

Uma lived happily on Mount Kailash with her husband and was content to always be by his side. Her husband's strange and unusual appearance and seemingly odd behaviour did not worry her because she knew in her heart how great and benevolent he was. She understood this king of mountains, his all-powerful mind, his infinite energy which cast its fiery light all over the world. But her father continued to hate him.

One day when Shiva, Brahma and many other gods were seated at a sacrifice ceremony Daksha entered. All those assembled rose to salute him except his father Brahma and Shiva. Daksha, an arrogant man, was very offended. He looked at Shiva angrily and said to the assembled gods, 'Though unwilling, I gave my daughter to this impure and proud abolisher of rites and demolisher of barriers. He roams about in dreadful cemeteries, attended by hosts of ghosts and sprites, like a mad man, naked with dishevelled hair, wearing a garland of dead men's skulls and ornaments of bones. To this wicked-hearted lord of the infuriate, whose purity has perished, I have, alas, given my virtuous daughter. This monkey-eyed god after having taken the hand of my fawn-eyed daughter has not, even by word, shown suitable respect to me, who he should have risen and saluted.' Shiva sat calmly listening to these insulting words. This made Daksha even more angry and rising to his feet, he cursed Shiva. 'Let this Bhava, lowest of the gods, never receive any portion during a sacrifice along with other gods.' Saying this he stormed out of the assembly.

This was the reason why they had not been invited to the great sacrifice but Shiva did not want to tell Uma this because he knew how fragile her heart was.

Uma grew more agitated as she watched the chariots go past. They were all going to her father's house, everyone in heaven except for her. Why should she stay here when all her sisters and other relatives were gathering in Daksha's house, she thought. She too would go. Her father must have forgotten to call her. When she told Shiva about her plans, he tried to stop her. 'Pray, beloved, do not go to your father's house. You are not wanted there. They will insult you. Please remain here in our mountain home which is so far from everyone,' said the great lord.

'Why should they insult me? My father will be happy to see me. I am his youngest and favourite daughter. He always loved me more than my sisters. I must go. I will go alone, my lord, if you do not wish to accompany me. I know you do not like to leave the mountains,' replied Uma and set out alone for her father's house. She arrived at Daksha's magnificent palace to find all other gods and goddess, demigods and her sisters were happily settled in but there was no one to welcome her. Uma went in search of her father, eager to see him. As she walked down the palace corridors, her sisters and their husbands followed her, laughing and ridiculing Shiva. 'Where is your great lord and master? Enjoying his ganja sleep, covered in ashes? Has he given you any jewels as yet or just a garland of skulls? Where are your ghosts?' Uma ignored them and ran to her father. She touched his feet and said, 'I rushed here, Father, as soon as I heard about the sacrifice. But why have you not called my lord Shiva to this great sacrifice? How can this ceremony take place without the supreme god?' she asked with tears in her eyes. Daksha flared up at once when he heard Shiva's name, 'Who was ever regarded Shiva as a god, leave alone the supreme god? Only you, my foolish child, were keen to marry him, this lowly creature who lives amongst the dead. You have lowered your dignity and my honour by becoming his wife. I do not want to insult my honoured guests with his lowly presence. I will never have his dark presence in my house,' said Daksha. Uma was stunned by her father's cruel words. She could not bear to hear him speak about Shiva, her beloved husband, in this demeaning way. Her heart was filled with pain. Bowing her head, she closed her eyes and thought of her husband. 'Lord, among all beings you are supreme in power because of your qualities. You are invincible, unapproachable because of your energy, fame and glory. Illustrious one, sinless one, great sorrow and trembling have come upon me because you have been denied your share in this sacrifice.' Saying this she gave up her life.

When Shiva heard that Uma had died he was filled with rage. His eyes blazed with anger and fire as he cursed Daksha. The lord of lords gathered his formidable powers and from the lock of his hair arose a gigantic thousand-armed demon. His head touched the skies and his feet dug into the nether world. His gaping mouth was filled with monstrous teeth dripping with blood. As this hideous giant named Virbhadra strode out, heaven and earth trembled with fear. Shiva commanded him to destroy Daksha and his sacrifice which had cost Uma her life. His fierce rage blazing like a forest fire, Shiva now charged down from Mount Kailash in a cloud of thunder and black smoke to destroy everything in his path. Reaching Daksha's palace with an army of giants, ghosts and sprites, he took hold of Daksha and tore his head from his body. The gods ran about trying desperately to escape Shiva's wrath and the sacrifice converting itself into a deer tried to flee but Shiva's arrow caught it.

When Shiva saw Sati's body lying dead on the ground he went mad with grief. His howls of anger and pain filled the sky till the mountains rocked and weeping he picked up Sati's body. His grief had turned him insane and he began walking with her body to the four corners of the earth. Blind with anger and sorrow, he danced in a frenzy of madness, scattering Sati's limbs and her ornaments all over the land. Wherever the various parts of the goddess's body fell, a shrine was built in her memory. As Shiva roamed the earth, his rage showing no signs of abating, the gods grew frightened. 'He will destroy us all if we do not stop him. But who will face his wrath? His burning gaze will turn him to ashes at once,' they said, their voices quivering with fear. Finally they went to Brahma and told him what had happened at Daksha's sacrifice ceremony. The lord of creation who had known what was to happen had not accepted Daksha's invitation. 'Go to Mount Kailash and ask for Shiva's forgiveness. He who is quick to anger is also easy to please. Recognize his true goodness. Know him as the supreme god and offer him your sincere prayers and share of sacrifice. This alone can help you stem his torrent of rage.' The gods rushed to Kailash where they found the great lord still immersed in deep sorrow, mourning for Sati. They fell at his feet crying for his forgiveness. In his greatness Shiva forgave them and even restored Daksha's head with a goat's head.

Then Vishnu spoke to him, 'O Shiva, recover your senses and listen to me. You will certainly find Sati, since you are as inseparable from her as cold from water, heat from fire, smell from earth or radiance from the sun.' As Shiva sat alone in his mountain home, Uma appeared to him bathed in a golden light. 'O Mahadeva, lord of my soul, in whatever state I exist I shall never be separated from my lord, and now I have been born as Parvati, daughter of Himavat, in order to become again thy wife. Therefore no longer grieve on account of our seperation.' Saying this she disappeared. Shiva remained still in deep meditation, calm and at peace, knowing Sati would become his wife again in her next life as Parvati.

Parvati was born in the home of the mountain god Himavat. When she was a young girl a sage came to their home and told her that she would one day marry an ascetic whose body was covered with ash. Parvati knew he meant that she was destined for Lord Shiva.

She soon grew up into a woman with such flawless
beauty and ethereal grace that even the gods fell in love
with her. Confident and somewhat proud, she declared
that she would only have Shiva as her husband. A
heavenly voice spoke to her, telling her she would have
to practise severe austerities to gain Shiva as her husband
but Parvati, proud of her great beauty and youth, just
laughed disdainfully. 'How can he not be my husband?
He who has mourned for me so long—how can he not
take me as a wife now that I am redolent of life? We
who have been predestined from our first being to be
husband and wife—how can any distance exist between
us,' she said, confident that Shiva would marry her as
soon as he set eyes on her lovely face. She continued to
play on the mountains, dance and sing with her friends,
quite secure about her future as Shiva's wife. But soon
her hopes were shattered. Shiva, she learnt to her dismay,
was totally immersed in deep meditation and none could
even approach the peak where he sat. Parvati asked the
god of love, Kama, to help her gain Shiva's attention.
'Once he opens his eyes and sees me he is sure to fall in
love with me. If you help me with your love darts then
surely I will not fail to win his heart. I am already his,
chosen by destiny. If he will only look at my face just
once.'

Kamadeva agreed to help the lovely Parvati and
began to work his magic at once. A soothing, warm

breeze began to blow and bees hummed a love song. Buds blossomed into flowers filled with sweet nectar and their fragrance filled the lonely mountain meadows where Shiva sat in meditation. At first nothing could break his concentration. Kamadeva's love magic began to cast its spell but the great god was not disturbed by its heady fragrance. Then Kamadeva picked up his bow and shot an arrow of love. There was such silence that it seemed as if the world had stopped moving. Slowly with intense anger Shiva opened his third eye to see who dared to disturb his meditation. His gaze, shimmering with fire, fell on Kamadeva who was right in his line of vision and the god of love was burnt to ashes in this fleeting ray of light. Without a glance at Parvati, Shiva then moved away to a higher place in the mountains where he could not be disturbed again.

Now Parvati, unhappy and distraught, remembered those heavenly words. 'Why did I, in my foolishness ignore those wise words. Now I shall punish this body of mine which was once so proud of its beauty.' And choosing a remote place in the mountains, she began to perform severe penance which lasted for many years. She, a young girl, outdid most great sages in practising austerities by living only on air and leaves. Soon she gave up eating leaves too and thus became known as Aparna, or one who shuns leaves.

When summer came and the sun blazed on her, she

lit four fires facing north, south, east and west and sat down in the centre of this burning circle with her eyes on the sun. In winter she sat in the ice-cold waters of a mountain lake, her delicate body turning blue with cold. Unaware of hunger or thirst, heat or cold, she meditated day and night on Shiva's memory, crying for his embrace. Her body became frail and the lustre of her golden skin faded like a fallen leaf.

One day an ascetic arrived at the place of her meditation and asked about her welfare. 'Why do you want to marry a god who has no riches, no palace of gold, no heavenly chariots? You, who are so beautiful, should not lack any suitors. Why should you, a jewel, throw yourself away? Shiva's face and body are terrible to behold and his habits are uncivilized and inauspicious. He is a beggar who lives in the land of dead bodies. O lovely, lotus-eyed maiden, pray do not marry such a distasteful character, I beg of you.'

At first Parvati ignored his words but then as he persisted in dissuading her from marrying Shiva, she rose angrily to reply. 'Who are you to speak thus of my lord? He is the core of my being. I belong to him and none else. Only he can claim me as his wife. He who is the lord of gods, on whom the crescent moon shines, who looks like the dark night touched by the light of the moon—my heart belongs to him. I shall marry only him,' she said and shut her eyes. Suddenly the mountain was ablaze with light as Shiva himself appeared before her. Frightened by his sudden presence, Parvati tried to move away but Shiva held her in his arms as the gods showered their blessings on them. Once more Shiva and Parvati were united as they were meant to be.

Lakshmi

Lakshmi

Lakshmi is one of the most sought after goddesses in Hindu mythology. Sri or Lakshmi, as depicted in the sacred texts, is the goddess of wealth and fortune, royal power and beauty. 'Sri-sukta', a hymn from the Rig Veda in praise of Lakshmi, gives a detailed description of her many virtues. She is invoked to bring fame and prosperity. She is bountiful and bestows upon her worshippers gold, cattle, horses and abundant food.

The hymn, one of the earliest dedicated to the goddess, associates many symbols with her. She is described as a beautiful goddess as lustrous as the moon who wears ornaments of gold and silver. Lakshmi is depicted seated on a lotus, her skin is the colour of a lotus in bloom and she wears a garland of lotuses too. Lakshmi, in fact, is often called Padma. Very often the goddess is shown in her Gajalakshmi image with elephants on either side showering her with water from their trunks.

Her other well-known forms are Rajyalakshmi where she is the companion of every ruler, a royal deity who protects the king as long as he remains true to the path of virtue but abandons him if he forsakes his princely duties and becomes an unworthy ruler. She is also known as Jayalakshmi, the goddess of victory, who changes sides as and when she wishes. Another popular form of the goddess is Grihalakshmi, the good, virtuous wife who takes care of her household with devotion.

She is also Bhagyalakshmi, the goddess of one's destiny and good fortune as well as Yasholakshmi, the goddess of fame. Her name is associated with all womanly virtues in Hindu tradition and newly-wed brides are often called 'Lakshmi' in the hope that she will bring good fortune to the household.

Lakshmi is worshipped throughout the year in a variety of festivals in cities as well as in villages. The most important festival associated with her is Deepavali when she is invoked to bring wealth and prosperity to the homes of her worshippers. Many Lakshmi devotees stay awake all night with the doors and windows of their houses open so that Lakshmi can enter and bless them with her presence. Since the goddess brings good fortune, on this day merchants and traders worship their account books too. A festival in rural Bengal celebrates the victory of Lakshmi, the good sister, over her sister Alakshmi, who is supposed to bring misfortune, poverty and hunger. A straw image is created and then destroyed with great fanfare and an image of Lakshmi is installed in her place.

By the late epic period (400 AD) Lakshmi became associated with Vishnu as his devoted wife. In Vishnu Purana we read, 'Sri, the bride of Vishnu, the mother of the world, is eternal, imperishable. As he is all-pervading so she is omnipresent. Vishnu is meaning, she is speech; he is polity, she's prudence; he understanding, and she intellect; he righteousness, and she devotion. In a word Vishnu is all that is called male and Lakshmi all that is termed female; there is nothing else than they.'

Though Lakshmi, being the goddess of fortune, is sometimes called fickle by devotees when she abandons them to poverty, her loyalty to Vishnu, her lord, is so steadfast that she is born as his wife in his various incarnations. The Vishnu Purana gives an account of her various names as the consort of Vishnu. 'As the lord of the worlds, the god of gods, Janardana descends amongst mankind in various shapes, and so does his consort Sri. Thus, when Hari was born as a dwarf, the son of Aditi, Lakshmi appeared from the lotus as Padma, or Kamala; when he was born as Rama (Parashurama) of the race of Bhrigu, she was Dharini; when he was Raghava (Ramachandra), she was Sita; when he was Krishna, she was Rukmini. In the other descents of Vishnu she was his associate. If he takes a celestial form, she appears as divine; if he is a mortal, she becomes mortal too, transforming her own person agreeably to whatever character it pleases Vishnu to assume.'

Lakshmi's first meeting with Vishnu is described in the legend of the churning of the ocean, which is given in detail in both the epics—*Mahabharata* and the *Ramayana*—as well as in the Vishnu Purana, Bhagavata Purana and Padma Purana. The following story is from the Vishnu Purana.

A sage named Durvaras was travelling when he met a celestial nymph who had a garland of fragrant flowers. The sage requested the maiden to give him the garland which she did at once. The sweet scent of the flowers intoxicated the sage and he began dancing with joy. Just then Indra, the lord of heaven, came by and the sage, in a benevolent mood, presented the celestial garland to him. Indra, unaware of the garland's mystical powers, threw it playfully on his elephant's head. The heady scent excited the elephant so much that he seized the garland with his trunk and cast it away. It flew in the air and fell on the ground. Sage Durvaras, furious at the way Indra had slighted his gift, cursed the lord of heaven. 'Your kingdom will be ruined,' he said. From then on Indra's powers began to wane. He begged the sage to forgive him but the curse would not leave him. Soon all the gods in heaven too began to lose their powers one by one and became afraid that the asuras would take over heaven. Feeble and fearful, they fled to Brahma for help. The lord of creation said he could not help them but Vishnu could perhaps find a way out of the crisis. The gods hastily went to Vishnu and pleaded for his help. Vishnu heard their plea and then told them what to do: 'Your strength shall be restored, only accomplish what I now command. Unite yourselves in peaceful combination with these your foes; collect all plants and herbs of diverse kinds from every quarter; cast them into the sea of milk, take Mandara the mountain for a churning stick, and Vasuki the serpent for a rope, together churn the ocean to produce the beverage-source of all strength and immortality. Then reckon on mine aid. I will take care. Your foes shall share your toil but not partake in its reward or drink the immortal draught.'

So the gods made friends with their enemies and started out at once to search for the precious herbs as Vishnu had told them to. The mountain Mandara agreed to help them and so did the serpent god Vasuki. 'But who will bear our combined weight?' they asked. Then Vishnu himself came forward in his gigantic tortoise form and on this pivot the churning began with great fanfare. The gods formed a line on one side while the demons took the other end of Vasuki and together they churned the ocean of milk with all their might. But to their shock the first gift that the ocean gave was a deadly poison. Shiva quickly swallowed it, thus saving the world from destruction. The poison remained in his throat, giving it a blue tinge and he was named Neelkanth, or the one with the blue throat, hereafter.

As the gods and the demons twisted and turned the serpent, many precious gifts arose from the ocean. Surabhi, the eternal fountain of milk; Varuni, the god of wine; Parijata, the tree of paradise, which filled the world with its fragrant blossoms; Ucchaishravas, the unique horse; Airavata, the divine elephant; and a bevy of beautiful apsaras emerged from the ocean along with many other precious gifts. Then emerged the goddess Lakshmi, seated on a lotus.

When she appeared the gods were enraptured and the heavenly choristers, the gandharvas, sang her praise while the apsaras danced around her. Ganga, the sacred river, followed her while heavenly elephants poured water over her. The ocean presented her with a garland of never-fading lotuses. Adorned with ornaments which the gods had presented to her, she rose from the ocean of milk, dazzling all who beheld her.

A poem from *Ramayana* (translated by Griffith) describes her with these lyrical words:

> When many a year had fled,
> Up floated, on her lotus bed,
> A maiden fair, and tender eyed
> In the young flush of beauty's pride.
> She shone with pearl and golden sheen,
> And seals of glory stamped her queen.
> On each round arm glowed many a gem,
> On her smooth brows a diadem.
> Rolling in waves beneath her crown
> The glory of her hair rolled down
> Pearls on her neck of price untold,
> The lady shone like burnished gold.
> Queen of the gods, she leapt to land,

A lotus in her perfect hand,
And fondly of the lotus sprung,
To lotus-bearing Vishnu clung,
Her, gods above and men below
As Beauty's Queen and Fortune know.

When Dhanvantari finally emerged from the ocean, carrying the pot of nectar, both the gods and the demons rushed to take it from his hands. Before the gods could reach him, the asuras, who were faster and more aggressive, carried away the vessel of amrita. The gods once more beseeched Lord Vishnu to come to their aid. Vishnu then took the form of a beautiful celestial maiden called Mohini. The demons had started quarrelling about who should drink the ambrosia first, and it was at this moment that Mohini appeared before them. The demons, overcome with passion, forgot their draught of immortality and rushed towards her. She offered to distribute the amrita equally amongst the demons. Totally bewitched by her beauty, they handed over the precious nectar to her. Mohini distributed the nectar to the gods and disappeared at once. Pandemonium broke loose but it was too late for the demons to do anything. They had been tricked out of immortality by Vishnu's maya. The lord of preservation was rewarded for his effort with Lakshmi who became his consort forever.

The following popular legend tells the story of how Rajyalakshmi takes sides according to her wishes.

Prahlad, the son of a demon named Virochana, was a good but meek king. Lakshmi, impressed with his princely virtues, decided to come and stay by his side but this made the gods uneasy. They asked Indra to request her to return to heaven. Lakshmi could not refuse him since he was the lord of heaven. As soon as she left Prahlad, his fortunes began to wane and all his royal might slipped away from him. He was soon reduced to a weak and impoverished ruler with no one to help him. Prahlad's son Bali realized why Lakshmi had left his father. 'The gods took her away because you were a meek, gentle and quiet king. They felt you did not deserve to have the goddess by your side. A king should be brave and valiant. He should go out to conquer the world. The goddess Lakshmi favours only those kings who are brave and valiant. I will show the goddess what a great king I can be and then surely she will return to us,' said Bali, who though virtuous like his father was also a formidable warrior. Soon, with a powerful combination of austere devotions and brave conquests, he had captured all the three worlds.

Once again the gods asked Vishnu to come to their rescue and save their heaven from Bali. Lord Vishnu then appeared before Bali, who was reigning in Indra's heaven, in the form of a dwarf Brahman, or his Vamana avatar. 'Welcome, O Brahman. What can we do for thee? Ask for me whatever thou desirest,' said the virtuous demon king. Vishnu, as the dwarf, then said to Bali, 'I ask from thee a small portion of ground, three paces measured step by step. I desire no more of thee. A wise man incurs no sin when he asks for as much as he needs.' Bali, though surprised at this small request, agreed at once. Then Vishnu assumed his cosmic form and took his first step which covered the entire earth. With his second step he reached across from one side of the heaven to the other. With his third step he could reach into the nether world but he stopped. 'Where shall I place my third step, O King,' he asked. Bali, who knew now that it was Vishnu who stood before him, bowed his head and said, 'Place thy foot upon my head. I fear not the nether world as much as a bad name,' and went away to live in the underworld. Indra regained his heaven and Lord Vishnu once more had goddess Lakshmi by his side.

The Devi Bhagavata Purana gives an account of the goddess Lakshmi being turned into a mare by Vishnu's curse.

Once due to some reason known only to Vishnu, he cursed his wife Lakshmi and turned her into a mare.

Though she was saddened by this she obeyed her husband and went away to live as a mare in the underworld. She chose a quiet, verdant forest where the two rivers Jamuna and Tamasa met and sat down to meditate. The goddess whose beauty glowed like the moon was content to be a mare since this was Vishnu's wish and she knew that he must have some reason to make her live in this form.

She began to meditate not on Vishnu but on Shiva, the god of the mountains. With a single-minded concentration she thought only of Shiva, the god with five faces and ten arms, whose glory was enhanced by his beautiful consort Parvati, whose pale body shone like moonlight, whose throat was marked blue with the poison he had swallowed, whose three eyes knew the three worlds, who wore an elephant's hide around his shoulders. She thought of the god who wore a garland of skulls around his neck and a gleaming serpent on his body. Days went by and seasons changed the forest from a canopy of green to a leafless, dry hill. Thousands of years passed as the goddess prayed to Shiva.

Then, pleased with her devotion, Shiva appeared before her one day. Riding his bull, he came to the sacred confluence of rivers with Parvati by his side. They beheld the goddess in her mare form and Shiva spoke to her. 'Why are you here, gentle woman? What need do you have to meditate? You are the beloved wife of Vishnu—

the lord of the universe, the one who grants everyone's wishes. Why do you leave such a supreme god and pray to me? The entire world prays to your husband who is the most benevolent of all gods and yet you think of me. Why is it so? A good wife should only serve her husband and your husband is the great god Vishnu. You must pray to him and not me,' said Shiva.

Lakshmi heard the words spoken by Shiva quietly and then she bowed to him and replied, 'O Lord! You who are so kind to your worshippers, I wish to tell you that my husband has cursed me. That is the reason I sit here on the banks of the rivers Jamuna and Tamasa in the form of a mare. That is why I pray to you day and night. Please release me from this curse. My lord said to me, "You shall return to me only after you have borne a son." Tell me, the lord with three eyes whose glance takes in the three worlds in one sweep, tell me how shall I have a son when my husband is not with me? When I am not in his care, how can I give birth to a child?' When Shiva did not reply to her she cast her eyes down and said, 'If you are pleased with my devotion then pray grant me a boon. There is no difference between my lord Vishnu and you. I have known this supreme truth ever since I have been with my lord. What you are, so is he and what he is, is the same as you. This is what is known to me and that is why I meditated and prayed to you.'

Then Shiva spoke. 'You are right. There is no difference between Vishnu and me. But how do you know this secret? Great sages have failed to come to this conclusion. How did you know this as the truth when it has confused so many of our devotees who see us as different forms? Tell me,' asked Shiva smiling at the goddess who had greatly pleased him.

Lakshmi replied, 'One day I was watching Vishnu who was in deep meditation. He sat alone totally detached from the world, his mind resting on a divine being. I did not disturb him but when he had finished his meditation and opened his eyes, his face gleaming with joy, I dared to ask him this question: "Lord, you who are a supreme god, above all other gods, it was you whom I chose when I rose out of the milk of ocean. I saw all the gods assembled there but you stood above them all. I realized then at once that you are the greatest of them all and that is why I chose to belong to you. But then who are you praying to? Who is above you in this world, my lord?" Vishnu, the lord of preservation replied thus to me, "Listen and I will tell you. With all my heart and mind I was meditating upon the image of Shiva, he who is so great yet so easily pleased. I was meditating upon him as he often meditates upon me. He is as dear to me as I am to him. We are bound together by a great love and there is no difference between us. Those who pray to me also pray to him and those who pray to me and do not show reverence to him shall never attain heaven." After Vishnu, my lord, had spoken these words to me I knew that you and he are the same so I prayed to you. I know that only you can lift the curse that is upon me and help me attain my husband once more,' said the goddess with tears in her eyes.

Shiva then placed his hand upon her head and spoke to her in a gentle tone. 'Be patient. Your wish will be granted. I am greatly pleased by your devotion and you will be reunited with your husband soon. When he hears my voice in his head, he will come here in the shape of a horse. You will be the proud mother of a beautiful son just as he had wished. The entire world will bow before this child and he shall rule the earth one day. After your son is born you shall return to Vaikunth once more with your husband and live there happily as his beloved wife.'

As Shiva had predicted, Vishnu came to meet Lakshmi in the form of a stallion. A son named Ekvir was born to her, who later became famous for his noble deeds.

Saraswati

Saraswati is one of the few important goddesses who has retained her glory from the Vedic age to the Puranic age and is still worshipped in many parts of India. At first she was known only as a river goddess and was associated in the Vedas with the mighty river Saraswati. Her name literally means 'the watery one'. There are frequent mentions in the Vedas that important rituals were performed on the banks of the river Saraswati. In the Rig Veda she is said to heal the god Indra along with the twin gods Asvins. During the later periods, Saraswati's connection with the river decreases and she begins to be invoked as Vagdevi—the goddess of speech. Her other names too describe her as a speech-deity and she is known as Jihvagravasini (dwelling in the front of the tongue), Kavijihvagravasini (she who dwells on the tongues of poets) and Mahavani (possessing great speech). Gradually Saraswati's benevolent powers began to encompass poetry, music and all creative arts and to this day this is how she is worshipped in many parts of India.

A hymn from the Rig Veda praises Saraswati with these words: 'Ye, opulent waters, command riches; ye possess excellent power and immortality; ye are the mistress of wealth and progeny; may Saraswati bestow this vitality on her worshipper' (Rig Veda vi. 52–6).

Saraswati is considered the muse of poets, artists and musicians and she is invoked by them whenever artistic excellence is desired. Even the gandharvas, the celestial singers and dancers, pray to her for inspiration before they sing or dance in the presence of gods. As a residing deity of the arts and learning, the goddess of wisdom, the mother of the Vedas, the inventer of the Devnagri script, prayers to Saraswati are offered every morning in schools and colleges in many parts of India.

The image of Saraswati in art is always serene and her colours are predominantly white and yellow, sometimes with a touch of blue to remind the devotee of her earlier image as a river goddess. She has four arms and holds a book, a veena, a rosary, and a water pot. The book is a symbol of learning, the veena associates her with musical arts while the rosary or string of pearls and the water pot are symbols of religious rites. Sometimes the goddess is depicted with two arms, seated on a lotus, playing the veena. Her mount is usually a pure white swan, its image matching the goddess in purity and serenity.

Saraswati is worshipped in the month of Magh (January) with a simple ritual, unlike her sister goddesses. Sometimes instead of an idol of the goddess, a book or a pen is worshipped, mostly by students. On the day of Saraswati Pooja, students are given a day off from learning and not allowed to write or read. The last watch of the night is considered especially sacred to Saraswati according to the Laws of Manu.

'Let the housekeeper awake in time sacred to Brahmi [one of her names, the feminine form of Brahma] goddess of speech, reflect on virtue and virtuous employments, and on the whole meaning and very essence of the Vedas.'

Saraswati, according to the Devi Bhagavata Purana, is one of the five dynamic female forces which emerged from the supreme spirit: 'Durga, Lakshmi, Saraswati, Savitri and Radha, these five goddesses are the spirit of Prakriti and the entire universal force emerges from these five. Listen Narada, in the beginning of creation Brahma divided himself into two—Prakriti and Purush. All the virtuous qualities of the great Creator are contained in these two forms.'

Krishna, the first complete Purush, in order to carry forth the act of creation, divides himself into male and female. The female form then further divides herself into five and Saras is one of these goddesses. Each goddess has a specific power and Saraswati is endowed with the creative force of knowledge and learning.

Saraswati's origin differs in the various Puranas. In the Matsya Purana Saraswati is said to have been born from Brahma when, desiring to create the world, he went into deep meditation.

Enraptured by his female self, who was Saraswati, Brahma desired her, mated with her and created the demigod Manu. In a folk myth based on this legend, Saraswati tried to escape her father's amorous attentions by running away. But she was not able to hide as he grew a head in whichever direction she fled. Some myths forgive Brahma this sin of incest by stating that he was fooled by Madana, the god of love, who was later burnt to ashes because of this misdeed. There are many other versions of this popular tale.

Saraswati's earlier origin can be seen in the Vamana Purana where her identity as the vedic river goddess is retained and she is said to be the presiding deity of thunder, clouds and rain.

Most puranic texts associate Saraswati with Brahma the Creator right from the time he began to form the universe. The Brahmavaivarta Purana says: 'When Brahma had fashioned all this universe, he placed his seed in Savitri [one of the names of Saraswati in this text] his best wife, as a man full of desire places his seed in a woman full of desire. For a hundred celestial years she held the embryo, which was difficult to bear, and then when she was ready to give birth she bore four enchanting Vedas; the various branches of knowledge such as logic and grammar; the thirty-six celestial Raginis that capture the heart; and the six beautiful Ragas with their various rhythms.'

A verse from the *Mahabharata* says: 'A voice derived from Brahma entered into the ears of them all; the celestial Saraswati was then produced from the heavens.'

But it is not Brahma who is her husband but Vishnu, according to the Skanda Purana. In this text it is mentioned that she emerged from Vishnu who held her on his tongue. Sometimes she is depicted as being his tongue. Because of her association with Vishnu many popular myths depict her as a jealous co-wife of Lakshmi which somehow goes against her serene, goddess-of-the-intellect image.

According to the Devi Bhagavata Purana Saraswati was the wife of Vishnu along with Lakshmi and Ganga. But in later mythology she becomes the consort of Brahma. This legend from the Devi Bhagavata Purana narrates how this came about.

The three lovely goddesses were all wives of Vishnu and lived in Vaikunth. While Lakshmi and Ganga were content and spoke lovingly to each other and to their husband, Saraswati was not happy about sharing the love and affection of her lord Vishnu. She followed the other wives with jealous eyes and soon began to believe that her husband loved Ganga much more than he loved her. Though this thought worried her all the time, she could not bring herself to complain to the lord. But as days went by her jealous heart grew more and more distraught and one day while the three of them were sitting together, she could no longer contain herself and suddenly rose up to accuse Ganga with these angry words: 'You have stolen my husband from me. He who used to have so much love for me, now he only looks at you.' Saying this she turned towards Lord Vishnu who had just entered the room. Her anger making her bolder than ever, Saraswati continued her tirade against Ganga. 'I know that she is the one you love now. Am I not your beloved wife too? Yet you have loving glances only for that one. You wish to see her by your side and not me.'

Vishnu, who loved his three wives equally, and did not wish to interfere in their quarrels, moved away ignoring her harsh words and this enraged Saraswati even more. Turning angrily towards Ganga she cried, 'Begone from my sight you wretched woman. You are a thief who has stolen my husband's love. He was my lord and you took him from me,' she said over and over again till poor Ganga could bear it no more and begged Vishnu to help her. But the lord of preservation remained calm and detached. His lotus eyes remained shut and his face was as still as a pool of water.

Then Lakshmi who had been sitting quietly, listening to Saraswati as she raged, decided to come to Ganga's rescue. 'Leave her alone. She has done you no harm.

Our lord loves us all equally. We three are blessed by his golden, benevolent light which falls impartially on us like the rays of the sun. O sister, I beg of you, leave Ganga alone,' said Lakshmi in her gentle voice. Her sweet words instead of calming Saraswati's anger made her even more furious and the goddess of learning now turned her fiery eyes towards her. 'How dare you take sides? You are my sister you say, yet I can see you love Ganga more than me. Both of you want me to leave so that you can share my husband's love between two of you instead of three of us. You are supposed to be my loyal sister but I will curse you today. You shall be born on earth as a plant.'

Lakshmi heard Saraswati's harsh words with a bowed head. She did not even lift her eyes to retaliate. She did not curse Saraswati in return though she could do so if she wished. She remained her calm and benevolent self, but her heart was touched by her sister's unhappiness and she moved forward to sooth Saraswati's angry brow. Though Lakshmi did not react to Saraswati's curse, Ganga, when she saw her beloved Lakshmi being berated by Saraswati, could not restrain herself. 'My true sister whom I love so dearly, who has never spoken an unkind word ever. I cannot bear it when this one so crazed with jealousy speaks like this to you. This Saraswati who cursed you will herself turn into a river. She will only flow in the dark crevices of hell where only evil men live,' said Ganga trembling with anger. These words made Saraswati flare up like a haystack on fire. She at once retaliated with another curse. 'You, the one who steals love which belongs to another woman, you with the sly eyes and a bee's sting will also flow in hell and on earth. You will turn into a river where men will wash their sins forever.' While the two goddesses raged with anger, Lakshmi sat in between as placid and calm as a moonbeam.

Then Lord Vishnu decided to put an end to this quarrel, and came into their midst once more, shining like a tower of gold. He called Saraswati to him and put his hand on her head affectionately to cool her temper. The lord of preservation already knew why they were quarreling and what the outcome would be. 'Beloved wife,' he said addressing the gentle Lakshmi first who sat with her eyes cast down. 'You will live on earth as the sacred plant Tulsi. But that will come later, first you shall descend to earth and live as the river Padmavati.' Then he turned to Ganga, 'You too will descend to the earth and flow as the river Bhagirathi. With your waters pure you will cleanse and release the souls of Bhagirath's kinsmen who are lying in hell.' Then finally the lord of preservation turned to Saraswati who now sat quietly by his side, full of remorse. 'You too will have to accept Ganga's curse and go down to the earth as a river. Later you will be worshipped for your skill in arts and

learning.' Then Vishnu looked at Lakshmi once more.
'Only she will return to me. She, who is the embodiment
of womanly grace and kindness. She who glows with
compassion, who is great and all forgiving. I have
immense respect for her because she is full of virtue.' As
Ganga and Saraswati bowed their heads, Lakshmi spoke
on their behalf. 'We will do as you say as it is our destiny.
But when will we be reunited with you? I must know
because I cannot exist without you. When will you rescue
me from my fate?' said the goddess of compassion and
placed her head on Vishnu's lotus feet.

Vishnu heard her plea and smiled at her. He
embraced her and said, 'I must keep my word and yet I
must be fair to all three. Saraswati, a part of you will
remain with me and another part will go to earth and
yet another part will go to Brahma and remain with
him. Ganga, you will go as I said to release the souls of
Bhagirath's kinsmen but before that you will have the
honour of living for a while on Shiva's head.' Then with
tenderness in his eyes Vishnu looked at Lakshmi. 'You
have to suffer the curse as it was ordained. Our
separation will be for a thousand years but after that
period you will return to me and we shall be together
forever.' Saying this, Vishnu left them to carry out their
destiny and journey to earth.

Another legend from the Skanda Purana tells us once more about the fiery temper of Saraswati. This time she leaves Brahma in a fit of anger. The story is narrated by Shiva to Parvati. Saraswati is known as Savitri here. A verse in Matsya Purana says she is called by several names, 'Brahma next formed from his immaculate substance a female who is celebrated under the names of Satrupa, Savitri, Saraswati, Gayatri and Brahmani.' Though in this legend from the Skanda Purana Savitri is the goddess Saraswati, Gayatri is another woman who causes a rift between Brahma and Saraswati.

'Listen, O Devi, and I will tell you how Saraswati forsook Brahma and he in consequence espoused Gayatri,' said Shiva to Parvati narrating the story.

Brahma along with Saraswati and many gods and holy sages went to Pushkar where a great sacrifice was being organized to bestow rain on the earth. All the preparations had been made to ensure that the rites and ceremonies went according to what had been prescribed by the gods. Suddenly some of the priests looked around and declared that Saraswati was not there. Brahma was surprised and he hastily sent a priest to call her. 'Tell her to come at once so that the ceremony is not delayed. The auspicious hour must not pass,' said the lord of creation. But when the priest returned he was alone. 'The Devi says she is not yet ready.' Another priest was sent to fetch her with an urgent message but he too came back without the goddess but with a message for the assembled gods. 'Tell them that I have not yet completed my dress nor arranged the household affairs. And moreover Lakshmi, Ganga, Indrani and the wives of other gods have not yet arrived so why should I proceed to the assembly with such unseemly haste?'

The priest then addressed Brahma. 'Saraswati is engaged and will not come; but without a wife what advantage can be derived from these rites?' Brahma, incensed at his wife's conduct commanded Indra, 'Hasten and in obedience to my order bring a wife from wherever you can find one.' Indra left the assembly at once and began to search for a suitable wife for Brahma. As he was walking, wondering where he would find such a woman, he saw a young and beautiful milkmaid, carrying a jar of butter. Her smiling face was glowing and her voice was soft as milk and honey. 'She will do,' he said and seizing her, brought her to Brahma at once. Brahma then addressed the assembly. 'O gods and holy sages, if it seems good unto you I will espouse this Gayatri, and she shall become the mother of the Vedas, and the cause of purity to these worlds.'

The milkmaid now known as Gayatri was arrayed in fine silken garments and bedecked with costly ornaments and led to the bower of the bride. In front of the entire assembly, the lord of creation was married to Gayatri.

At this very moment when the wedding vows were complete, Saraswati, her various chores done, finally arrived at the assembly accompanied by the wives of Vishnu, Shiva and other gods. She was filled with rage when she saw the milkmaid in the bridal bower, glittering with jewels. Overcome with anger, she could not speak for a moment and then angry words rushed from her like a river in flood. 'O Brahma. You have rejected me, your wedded wife, for this milkmaid. Have you no sense of shame to discard me like this? You, who are called the great father of gods and holy sages— how could you commit such a sinful act which will shock all the three worlds? O Lord, how can I show my face to the world now that you have forsaken me? Deserted by my husband, I can no longer call myself a wife.' Brahma heard her angry speech calmly and when she had finished he replied, 'Calm yourself, wife. I did so because the priests informed me that the time for the sacrifice was passing away and that it could not be performed properly unless my wife was present with me. Indra brought Gayatri along and Rudra and Vishnu gave her in marriage to me. Devi, forgive this one act of mine which has caused you so much anger and pain. I will never offend you again.'

But Saraswati could not be appeased so easily. She looked around the assembly, her beautiful eyes blazing with fire, and cursed each and every one of the gods.

First to hear the words of rage was Brahma himself. 'May you never be worshipped in a temple except for one day in a year. Indra, since you brought that milkmaid to Brahma, you shall be bound in chains by your enemies.' Then she turned to Vishnu and said, 'You are the one who gave her in marriage to Brahma so you shall be born amongst men and for long you will wander as the humble keeper of cattle.' To the priests and sages who had witnessed the marriage of Brahma, she said, 'Henceforth you shall perform sacrifices solely from the desire of obtaining gifts, from covetousness shall you attend holy places.' The wives of the gods assembled could not escape her wrath either though they were just innocent bystanders and she raged at them, 'May you all remain barren.' After having pronounced her torrent of curses Saraswati stormed out of the assembly. Vishnu tried in vain to appease her but the goddess would not listen to him and left. The curses were then modified by Gayatri who gave the assembled gods her blessings.

The Padma Purana gives a different and happier ending to the story.

Brahma did not want Saraswati to leave in such a rage and asked Vishnu and Lakshmi to go with her. 'Ask her to return. Calm her down with soothing words.' After much cajoling, Saraswati's anger finally cooled down and she returned to the assembly of gods. Vishnu had succeeded in appeasing the goddess so well that soon she became her benevolent self and was kind enough to modify her curses. She was then persuaded to give her blessings to all those assembled and Gayatri, who had been standing quietly till now, came and fell at Saraswati's feet. The goddess raised her up and embracing her said, 'A wife ought to obey the wishes and orders of her husband; for that wife who reproaches her husband and who is complaining and quarrelsome shall most assuredly when she dies go to hell. Therefore let us both be attached to Brahma.' Gayatri, happy that the goddess of learning had forgiven her, said, 'So be it. Your orders will I always obey, and esteem your friendship precious as my life. Your daughter am I, O goddess! Deign to protect me.'

Sita

For centuries, Sita, the heroine of the *Ramayana*, has been the role model for an ideal Hindu wife. One of the most popular heroines in both classical literature and art and in folklore, Sita is revered as a self-sacrificing, loyal wife who is steadfast in her love for her husband despite many hardships.

A tragic heroine of mythology, Sita's life was never easy even in her previous births. Her name Sita means 'furrow' or a 'line made by the plough' and in Vedic literature she was seen originally as a goddess of agriculture. In a hymn from the Rig Veda Sita is invoked with these words:

'Auspicious Sita, come thou near:
We venerate and worship thee
That thou mayst bless and prosper us
and bring us fruits abundantly

May Indra press the furrow down,
may Pushan guide its course aright.
May she, as rich in milk, be drained for us
through each succeeding year.
(from *Hindu Goddesses*)

Though her name was invoked during various Vedic rituals and the goddess was associated with thunder and rain, Sita became an important goddess after Valmiki's

Ramayana. It is clear in the epic that Sita was not an ordinary mortal and even her birth was 'ayonija', or 'not from a womb'. Since she is the consort of Rama, an avatar of Vishnu, Sita is considered an avatar of Lakshmi in the *Ramayana*.

Rama, as it is destined, wins Sita at her swayamvara, a contest for suitors to win the bride, and brings her to Ayodhya as his wife. She follows him to the forest when he is banished, sharing the life of deprivation with him and later when she is abducted by Ravana, she remains chaste and loyal to her husband. Sita's purity, sacrifice and devotion to Rama elevated her position in the galaxy of goddesses, and now she stands on a high pedestal— an ideal Hindu wife. Though she is never depicted as a powerful goddess like Durga or an independent one like Lakshmi and there are probably no temples dedicated only to her as she is rarely worshipped in her own right, she still remains a popular figure of wifely devotion and loyalty. Every child knows the story of her selfless devotion to Rama, and women are praised for being a 'Sita-like wife'. A verse from the *Ramayana*, which was spoken for Sita, is sung during wedding ceremonies when the father gives the bride away:

'Here is my daughter, Sita, who will forever walk with you on the path of dharma. Take her hand. Blessed and devoted, she will ever be with you like your own shadow.'

In north India, every autumn, the story of *Ramayana* is enacted during Ramlila. The role of Sita is played by male actors, and whenever she appears on stage the spectators throw flowers at her feet. Sometimes she is addressed as the mother, who leads her devotees to Rama.

Despite her subordinate position, Sita is depicted as a woman with great strength of character who bore her misfortunes with long-suffering patience and finally decided to depart with dignity from this earthly life.

As an incarnation of Lakshmi, Sita is said to have been born again to take revenge on Ravana who had insulted her in her previous birth. Sita's extraordinary birth is described in this story from the *Ramayana*.

Ravana, in the course of his wanderings through the world, came to a forest on the Himalayas, where he saw a damsel of brilliant beauty. She was dressed in the robes of an ascetic and lost in deep meditation. Ravana, enamoured by her beauty and simplicity, tells her that she who is so young and desirable should not be leading a life of austerity. 'Who are you? Why are you here, in this lonely place?' he asked her. After some hesitation she replied, 'I am Vedavati, the daughter of sage Kusadhvaja, sprung from him during his constant study of the Vedas. The gods wished that I should choose a husband, but my father would give me to none else than to Vishnu, the lord of the world, whom he desired for a son-in-law.' This resolution by Vedavati's father had made many gods and kings angry. 'Only Lord Vishnu will do for him. Does the sage, in his arrogance, think us inferior,' they had muttered. Sambini, the king of the rakshasas, was so enraged by this that he killed sage Kusadhvaja while he was asleep. Vedavati's mother, overcome by grief at the loss of her husband, embraced his body and entered the fire. 'In order that I may fulfil this desire of my father in respect of Narayana (Vishnu), I wed him with my heart. After having done so I practise great austerity. I resort to this severe observance from the desire of obtaining him,' said Vedavati returning to her meditation.

But Ravana was not thwarted by her words and pressed his suit. His passion was not diminished even though Vedavati refused to look at him. He told her only old people should practise austerity. 'You who are so young and beautiful should become my wife. I am Ravana—a great king and superior to Vishnu,' he boasted. Vedavati replied that no one can stand before Lord Vishnu and chided him for speaking thus about her lord. Ravana refused to leave and moved forward to touch her hair with the tip of his finger. Vedavati, greatly incensed, cut off her hair at once. 'You vile man. You have insulted me by touching the hair on my head with your finger. You have shamed me and I can no longer continue to live. I shall enter into the fire at this

very moment before your eyes. But hear my word, O
arrogant king. Since I have been insulted in the forest
by you who are wicked-hearted, I shall be born again
for your destruction. For a man of evil design cannot be
slain by a woman, and the merit of my austerity will be
lost if I were to launch a curse against you. But if I have
performed, or bestowed, or sacrificed aught, may I be
born a virtuous daughter, not produced by the womb,
of a righteous man.' Having thus spoken she entered
the blazing fire and a shower of celestial sparks fell from
the sky.

The verse then explains the birth of Sita to Rama.
'She it is, lord, who has been born as the daughter of
King Janaka and has become thy bride; for thou art the
eternal Vishnu. The mountain-like enemy who was
virtually destroyed before by her wrath has now been
slain by her, having recourse to thy superhuman energy.'

Vedavati was born again as Sita. As predicted, her
birth was not from the womb but from the earth itself.
King Janaka of Mithila, a nobel and virtuous ruler, and
a learned king who Krishna cites in the Bhagavad Gita
as an illustrious example of a Karma Yogi, was chosen
by the gods to be worthy of Sita's father. One day he
was ploughing his fields himself to prepare for a sacrifice
when he suddenly saw a beautiful girl spring up from
the furrow. Janaka accepted the child as goddess earth's
gift to him and named the infant girl Sita.

A folk variation of this legend gives an interesting account of how Sita came to be born from the earth.

Vedavati, daughter of sage Kusadhvaja, was born from his mouth while he was chanting the Vedas. She was the incarnation of Lakshmi and soon after she was born her parents regained all the wealth and prosperity they had lost earlier. From an young age she wanted Lord Vishnu to be her husband and prayed to him every day.

An asura named Sambhu came to the hermitage one day and asked her to marry him but when her father did not give his consent, the asura killed him. When Vedavati saw her father lying in a pool of blood, she looked at the asura with anger and rage and he was burnt to ashes at once. Then Vedavati went away to the mountains and began to do severe penance to get Vishnu as her husband.

This was the time when Ravana had begun his campaign of conquests all over the earth. Like a raging fire he stormed through the land, defeating all kings in his way. When he reached the Himalayas, he saw the beautiful Vedavati sitting alone on a mountain peak. He fell in love with her at once and asked her who she was and what she was doing in such a remote place all alone. When Vedavati did not respond to him he boasted, 'I am the mighty ten-headed king of Lanka, Ravana. I have come here after defeating all the kings that stood in my way. I desire to make you my wife. Throw away your garments of bark, let your matted tresses be beautiful again. Adorn yourself in silk and gold. Come with me beautiful maiden. This life is not for you.' His words made no impression on Vedavati who sat quietly chanting her lord's name. Ravana lost his temper and tried to pull her hand. Vedavati immediately bit his hand and fled from the spot.

'You have defiled me and I no longer wish to retain this body touched by your vile hands,' she said and burnt herself right before his eyes. 'I will be born again. Lord Vishnu will be my husband and I will be the cause of your death,' she vowed before she died.

Ravana was astounded by Vedavati's death. 'How lovely she was. I wanted her to be my queen,' he said feeling extremely sad for himself. Then he collected the ashes from the ground with his own hands while his army generals watched in amazement. When he reached Lanka he ordered a golden box to be made in which he put Vedavati's ashes. He chose a quiet place in his palace garden to bury it and used to visit the bower every day to pay his respects to Vedavati. But bad omens began to be seen in Lanka after the arrival of Vedavati's ashes. Floods, famine and death took over the city. One day Narada arrived at the palace and he told Ravana that the cause of these bad omens and ill luck was the golden box of ashes. 'If you keep that box here any longer it will cause great destruction and disaster for your land,' he announced. Ravana's queens, horrified at the thought of the evil shadow the box was casting over their empire, begged him to throw it away. With a heavy heart, Ravana took the golden box of Vedavati's ashes and cast it into the sea. The waves carried the box to the shores of India, where it lay buried in the sand. Then one day, a gang of robbers found the box and carried it away to a forest in the northern part of India. When they were caught by the king's soldiers, one of them hid it under the roots of a tree, hoping to retrieve it later. But the next day the river flooded the forest and the box was carried away to Mithila where it lay under the river basin for some years. This was the very place chosen by King Janaka for a sacrifice. The ashes of Vedavati had mingled with her spirit and formed a female child and this was the child that Janaka found and named Sita.

The story of Sita's wedding to Rama is narrated at great length in the *Ramayana* and in the Devi Bhagavata Purana. In later periods poets such as Tulsidas wrote beautiful verses describing this episode. Many popular folk tales in various languages celebrate this well-loved story and ballads are sung in villages all over India during

the Dussehra festival. 'Sita Swayamvar' attracts a huge
crowd when it is enacted during Ramlila and women
offer sweets to each other when the wedding takes place
on stage.

When Rama was about sixteen years of age, a sage
named Vishwamitra came to his father, King Dasarath,
and asked his help to kill two demons named Maricha
and Suvahu. Rama and his younger brother Lakshmana
set out with the sage to his hermitage in the forest. They
soon put an end to the demons and the sage, pleased
with them, offered them many boons. The hermits told
Rama that they had been invited to a sacrifice which
King Janaka of Mithila had organized and asked Rama
and Lakshmana to accompany them. They told Rama,
who was uncertain about going with them, about the
mighty bow which King Janaka possessed. 'A bow which
belonged to Shiva himself. It was with this bow that
Shiva had created havoc when enraged at the way Sati
had been treated by her father Daksha. The bow was a
gift from Shiva to Janaka—a reward for a sacrifice.
Janaka had declared that he would only give his daughter
Sita's hand in marriage to the man who could string
this great bow of Shiva's.'

Rama was thus persuaded to accompany the sages
to Janaka's court. When the two princes arrived, Janaka
was very pleased to see them and offered them the best
seat in his court. He showed them the mighty bow and
said, 'This heavenly bow, if young Rama's hand can

string, to him I shall give, as I have sworn, my daughter Sita, who was not born of a woman.'

The king ordered his men to bring the bow which was kept in an iron box. It was brought to the assembly on an eight-wheeled carriage, a row of men pulling it like a chariot. All the kings and princes gathered at Janaka's court gasped at its immense weight. Those who had some pride decided that they would not even attempt to lift it but some foolish and vain princes strutted up to the box, tightening their belts. One by one they all failed and returned to their seats, their faces burning with shame. Kings, princes, gods and demons in the form of mortal men, they all came and tried their hand but the bow seemed to get heavier. It seemed as if Brahma had not created a single man who could move the bow, leave alone lift and string it.

'I know now that this earth is bereft of brave men. If only I had known this I would have not made this pledge. Now my daughter will remain unmarried because I cannot change my words and lose face,' declared Janaka with sorrow. The entire assembly looked at Sita, seated like a lotus bud amongst them, and felt her father's sadness in their hearts.

When he heard these words, Lakshmana's lips quivered with anger but fearing his older brother he swallowed his words. He laid his head at Rama's feet and said, 'O Rama, how dare anyone utter these words in your presence? Does he not know that you can pick this bow as easily as a lotus stem?' Rama placed his hand on Lakshmana's head with affection and stayed calmly seated. Then Vishwamitra spoke to him. 'Rise, O Rama. Break this mighty bow of Shiva and erase Janaka's plight.' Hearing these words Rama bowed his head to his guru. There was no elation in his heart neither was there any agitation. He stood up and walked towards the bow as graceful as a young lion. Silence fell on the assembly. The sages began to offer prayers in their minds. Sita sat quietly, her heart full of fear and love for Rama. She began to call upon all the gods she could recall at that moment with an agitated mind. 'O Shiva, please shower your blessing on me and take away the weight of this bow. O Ganesha, you give us all boons. Please take away the weight of this bow,' she said over and over again, her eyes filling with tears. 'Why did my father keep such a difficult pledge? This is so unfair. Behold this bow which is like a bolt of lightning and this tender lotus-eyed, dark-skinned boy. How can I sit here patiently and watch what is going to happen? Can a soft siris blossom pierce a diamond? Has everyone lost their senses? O Shiva's mighty bow, now you are my only hope. Cast your heaviness away to the winds and help me,' thought Sita, her eyes restlessly darting about like fish in a pond. Then realizing that her tears would not stop and her heart would not stay calm, Sita spoke these soothing words to herself to quieten her fears: 'If I am true in my spirit, body and words to my lord, then the god who lives in everyone's heart will certainly make me my Lord Rama's slave.' Sita looked at Rama and then cast her eyes down to the ground. 'Those who have true love in their heart will always win the one they love, there is no doubt about that.' She looked at Rama again and decided in her heart to be only his, come whatever may. The moment her shy glance, brimming with love, fell on Rama's face, he knew what was on her mind.

With a quick movement full of grace, he opened the iron box and lifted the bow effortlessly as if it were a garland of flowers. The bow crackled like lightning and its form filled the sky in a blaze of silver. Not one person in the huge assembly saw Rama lift the bow or string it since he moved as swiftly as light, but they heard the roar of thunder that made them tremble with fear. A deafening noise echoed through all the three worlds, the sun's horses left their path and began to run helter-skelter, wild beasts began to howl as the earth swayed. Then everyone cried out 'Hail Rama'. From the sky, music began to play as the apsaras sang and danced.

Sita's happiness knew no bounds as she walked

towards Rama, holding the nuptial garland. Though her
shyness made her timid, her love for Rama made her
heart leap with joy. She knew that her love for him was
a secret as yet from her family and none could see it in
her heart. But when she reached Rama, Sita was so
dazzled by him, that she stood mute, unable to move.
Her friends cleverly guessed the turmoil in her heart
and whispered, 'O lovely Princess, put the garland
around his neck.' Sita, shaken out of her trance, tried to
lift her hands but was suddenly so overwhelmed by love
that she could not raise her arms. Then as the women
began to sing in praise of Rama, Sita managed to put
the garland around her beloved Rama with trembling
hands. Once more the heavens filled with music as
flowers streamed down over the wedded pair. The earth,
sky and the underworld rejoiced when they heard that
Rama had broken the mighty bow and won Sita's hand.
In every home, rich and poor, people lit lamps to show
their happiness, while Brahma and a host of other
celestial beings showered their blessings on Rama and
Sita.

In the *Ramayana*, as well as in other literature from
Hindu mythology, Sita is defined as the ideal wife, whose
entire life revolves around her husband. For Sita, Rama

is the very essence of life and she always remains faithful to him. Sita's loyalty and devotion to Rama as a 'pativrata' is illustrated by several episodes in the *Ramayana*.

Rama was exiled to the forest for fourteen years. As he prepared to leave, obeying his father's orders, he told Sita that she could not accompany him as she would not be able to bear the harsh life of the forest. 'You have only known the comfort of a palace and you will not be able to bear the ordeals of a forest life.' Sita, grief-stricken at the thought of life without Rama, said, 'O son of an illustrious monarch, a father, a mother, a brother, a son or a daughter-in-law enjoy the fruit of their merits and receive what is their due, a wife alone follows the destiny of her consort. From now on my duty is clear, I shall dwell in the forest! For a woman, it is not her father, her son, nor her mother, friends nor her own self, but the husband, who in this world and the next is ever her sole means of salvation. If you do enter the impenetrable forest today, O descendant of Raghu, I shall precede you on foot, treading down the spiky kusha grass . . . I shall dwell as willingly in the forest as formerly I inhabited the palace of my father, having no anxiety in the three worlds and reflecting on my duties towards my lord. Ever subject to your will, docile, living like an ascetic in those honey-scented woodlands, I shall be happy in your proximity, O Rama, O Illustrious Lord.'

Rama tried to dissuade her, telling her that it was not safe for her to be in the forest where there were wild beasts and demons and he could not bear to inflict such a hardship on her. 'I have to obey my father's wishes, but why should you give up your comfortable life here. You will be safer and happier living in the palace with your father-in-law and mother-in-law instead of living a harsh life in the forest with me,' he said. But Sita though docile and timid showed a firm resolve which astounded everyone. 'The hardships described by you will be transmuted into joys through my devotion to you. If I am ever separated from you I shall immediately yield up my life. Without her consort, a woman cannot live, you cannot doubt this truth where I am concerned. O pure-souled one, I shall remain sinless by following piously in the steps of my consort, for a husband is a god.'

Thus Sita convinced Rama to allow her to go with him. They lived in the forest happily for a while, enjoying the simple life in their hut in Chitrakoot. Then one day Ravana's shadow fell once more on Sita. She was abducted by him and taken to Lanka.

This episode from the Ramacharitmanas describes Sita's grief at being parted from Rama.

Abducted by Ravana and taken to Lanka, Sita was kept as a prisoner in a garden full of ashoka trees.

Sita sat under the shade of an ashoka tree with her eyes downcast and her heart filled with sorrow. She did not look up when Ravana, accompanied by his wives, came and stood before her. 'Raise your eyes, lovely woman. Look up at me just once and I will give you all the wealth in the world. My love for you is limitless. I have everything in the world, wealth, fame, power yet I humble myself before you. I am the king of demons and I could take you by force, but I do not want to do that. Agree to be mine. I will make these queens of mine your slaves. Marry me and you will be the queen of the world,' he said, but Sita did not lift her face. 'Marry me, you proud and obstinate woman, or else I will kill you,' he roared. Sita then spoke in a quiet voice, keeping her face hidden from Ravana. 'Can a lotus flower in the light of a lowly glowworm? You evil man, have you no fear of Lord Rama's lethal arrow? You have brought me here by deceit. You are not a mighty king but a coward who steals helpless women when their menfolk are away. Are you not ashamed of yourself? Even a snake is better than you that crawls on the ground.' Ravana was stunned by Sita's insulting words. None had ever dared to speak to him like this and abuse him in the presence of his queens. He drew his sword in fury and rushed towards Sita. 'I will kill you here and now, you have insulted me. Listen woman, marry me at once, or I will cut your head off and slice your body into pieces with this sword of mine which has seen only victory in battle.'

'Kill me then,' said Sita, 'I will prefer to die by this cold and clean sword to suffering this terrible fire of agony which has been burning in me ever since I have been separated from my lord.' As Ravana was about to raise his sword, his wife Mandodari stopped him. 'It is wrong for you—a great warrior—to slay a woman. It is against all norms. Restrain your anger, mighty King of Lanka. Remember your glory in this kingdom of yours,' she said.

Though Ravana was fuming with rage he had to listen to his wife's wise words. He looked down at Sita angrily and said, 'I give you a month to make up your mind to marry me. If you do not agree, you will be put to death,' and stormed out of the ashoka garden. As soon as he left, all the demonesses who had been left to guard Sita began harassing her, whispering cruel words into her ears. They took on horrible forms and attacked her from all sides, trying to frighten her into accepting Ravana's proposal. Sita covered her face in her arms and meditated upon an image of Rama. Her doe eyes which had been filled with tears gradually cleared as she thought of her beloved Rama and her heart, though heavy with sorrow, felt joyous as her mind shone with her lord's form.

Just then one of the demonesses, Trijata, who secretly worshipped Rama, came forward and spoke to the others. 'Gather around me and listen. I had a dream last night which you should pay attention to because it will soon come true. I dreamt last night that a giant of a monkey has burnt our Lanka and killed our entire army of mighty demons. Ravana, our king, is naked and all his heads are shaven. I saw him heading towards the land of the dead, riding a donkey, his twenty arms cut off. As he leaves, I saw Vibhishan being crowned our king and the entire land singing Rama's name. Then the lord calls Sita to him. Believe in this dream of mine because I swear it will come true within a few days.'

When the demonesses heard Trijata's words, they were frightened and fell at Sita's feet, asking for her forgiveness. Then they all ran away, leaving Sita alone in the ashoka garden with only Trijata. Sita, afraid that a month would soon be over, asked Trijata to help her. 'You are my friend in this hour of my ordeal. Help me, kind friend, to put an end to this endless life of sorrow. Bring some firewood and make a funeral pyre and light it for me. I cannot bear to hear Ravana's voice again.' Trijata touched Sita's feet and soothed her with kind words. She reminded her of Rama's glory, strength and valour and then, as night fell, she went away leaving Sita alone.

'What shall I do to end this burden of grief? Where shall I get the fire to erase this sorrow?' cried Sita looking up at the night sky. 'The sky is filled with flames but not one star falls on earth. The moon too is full of fire but it does not shower its burning arrows on an unfortunate woman like me. Listen to me, O ashoka trees. Take my sorrow away so that you become true to your names. Your tender green leaves are like embers of fire. Shower them on me and reach this grief to its end.'

Hanuman, who had been hiding in the trees till then, threw her a ring which belonged to Rama. Sita, thinking the ashoka tree had thrown her a bit of flame, put her hand out quickly and picked it up. When she saw it was Rama's ring, her heart leapt with joy at first and then was filled with fear. 'How can his ring be here? No, nothing can happen to my lord. He is invincible in this world, who can defeat him? But who can make a ring like this which only belongs to him?' Anxious thoughts raced through Sita's mind. Then Hanuman, who knew now that he had to convince Sita of Rama's well-being, began singing Rama's praises. He sang sweetly of all the noble deeds Rama had done from the time he was a young boy. He sang about Rama's great beauty, his valour, and as soon as Sita heard the words describing her husband's glory, her heart was at peace. 'Come forward whoever you are. Why do you not show yourself?' she asked, looking up at the ashoka trees. Hanuman jumped down to reveal himself, much to Sita's surprise. What was this? A monkey who sang her lord's praises? Where has he come from, she thought. Hanuman, by then certain that this was Sita and no other, came and bowed before her. 'O Mother Sita, I am your Lord Rama's messenger. He gave me this ring to give to you,' he said and explained how he had come to meet Rama. Once Sita knew that Hanuman was truly Rama's messenger, she began asking him about her lord.

'O Hanuman, I was drowning in this sea of grief but you have appeared like a ship to save me. Tell me, does my lord think of me? Will my eyes ever find solace in that dark, gentle image?' Sita was choking with sorrow and her eyes filled with tears. 'O my lord, have you totally forsaken me?' she cried. Hanuman could not bear to see Sita's grief and spoke to her in a gentle voice. 'He is well in body but his heart is full of sorrow. Do not make yourself unhappy. Rama's love for you is as great as yours for him. Have patience and listen to his message which I will now relate to you, mother,' and folding his hands in prayer Hanuman began to recite Rama's message to Sita. 'These are his words spoken for you, "O Sita, in your absence everything has turned contrary for me. The new leaves of a tree are like flames, the gentle moon like the fierce sun, a lotus blossom as sharp as a spear. It seems to me as if the clouds are pouring boiling oil on earth and those who cared for me once now only make me suffer. The fragrant, cool winds that once blew in this land have now become hot and poisonous. They say that if you speak of your grief to someone it may become easier to bear it, but who will I speak to. There is none who knows the intensity and depth of our love except my mind, and my mind is forever with you, my love. With this, understand in your heart the love I have for you."'

When Sita heard these words, she was so overwhelmed with love for Rama that she forgot everything and lost herself totally, thinking of her beloved Rama. Then she opened her tear-filled doe eyes and spoke to Hanuman, 'You bring me a message which gives both bliss and pain. Bliss, because I still abide in his heart; pain, as he wakes and weeps far from me.'

When Sita was finally rescued by Rama and Lakshmana and their vast army of valiant monkeys, instead of a joyous meeting with Rama, she was greeted coldly by her husband. In this episode from the *Ramayana*, Sita is made to go through an ordeal by fire to prove her innocence.

After the battle was over, Sita waited. This was the moment she had longed for. But why was it not as joyous as she had envisioned it would be? Rama, who she thought she would never see again, for whom her heart cried every night, stood before her like a stranger. It was as if he had never seen her before and had nothing to do with her. He gazed upon her and spoke in an unfamiliar, cold voice. 'I have won you, fair lady, by conquering my enemy in battle,' said Rama. 'I have obliterated the dishonour that was upon me and vanquished my enemy with the help of these brave monkeys. Today the black shadow cast upon my family honour has been erased. I have done all that a man should do to wipe out an intolerable insult at the hands of an enemy. I won you, Sita, as every man should fight to protect his wife. But let it be known that this great battle accomplished by means of heroism of my friends was not undertaken by me for your sake. It was not love for you that led my army over the sea. I battled to avenge the cause of honour and insult.'

Sita looked at him, bewildered by his harsh words. Could this really be true, she thought, gazing upon her husband. 'Is this really his voice that attacks me thus like a shower of arrows? Why does he speak these harsh words to me before this vast army of monkeys and demons?' Then Rama continued, keeping his face averted from her face. 'But as you stand before me, doubts have arisen about your behaviour. What man of good family can take back his wife after she has lived in another man's house for so long? Should he compromise his honour, his family's good name just because he longs for her? Sita, go away from me. Go and live wherever you wish but do not stand before me. I no longer wish to see you.'

Sita, deeply ashamed and trembling with sorrow, tried to speak to him. Her beautiful face was wet with tears and Rama's voice, harsh and unfamiliar, echoed in her ears, filling her with a deep sadness.

Then he spoke to her again. 'Go. Go at once. Choose any place and I will see you are reached there. Just understand that you cannot live with me. You may be my wife but you have lived under Ravana's care for so long. He must have gazed upon your beautiful face so many times, tried to put his arms around your waist. You are tainted by his evil touch. I cannot accept you as my wife any more. Leave me since I do not wish to see you ever again.'

Sita stood still as her husband accused her with these cruel words in front of the entire army. Her eyes full of tears, she tried once again to speak to Rama, to tell him that she was innocent. 'Why do you accuse me in this heartless way? I have done no wrong. I am as chaste and pure as I always was. Believe me, my lord, I have not behaved in any improper way. My heart is ever attached to you. My eyes see nothing but your face. My ears hear no voice but yours. Do not cast me aside like this. I cannot live without you,' she cried, but Rama turned his face away. 'If you wanted to discard me why did you send Hanuman with your ring? Why did you give me hope to live on? I was quite willing to die when my heart was breaking with sorrow, when I thought I would never set eyes upon you again. I know now that death is the only way out for me. Discarded by you, tainted by false accusations, I do not wish to live. Build a pyre for me. By entering the fire I will end this life of sorrow. Fire shall be my solace,' said Sita.

Lakshmana and Hanuman, who were standing nearby, tried to persuade Rama to take Sita back. 'She is as pure as the earth and the sky,' they said, but Rama showed no signs of forgiving her. He ordered Lakshmana to build a pyre for Sita. As the monkeys and demons watched, Sita folded her hands and prayed to the fire. 'As my heart never wavered for even a moment from the image of Rama, fire that purifies all, protect my honour.' And then she walked around the pyre and stepped into the blazing fire.

As soon as the flames touched her body, all the people who were watching, the army of monkeys and rakshasas began to wail loudly. Lakshmana, Hanuman and many of the vanquished demons too cried out in horror. They begged Rama to save Sita from this cruel fate. But Rama did not even look towards the burning pyre.

But as the fire burned, sending its flames high into the sky, they saw an amazing sight. Sita sat in the middle of the raging fire but somehow her beautiful form remained intact. The flames rose around her in a golden circle but they did not touch her. Her lovely face, her graceful body, her hair shone as before and her clothes too retained their lustre. One by one the gods began to descend from heaven. Kubera, Yama, Indra, Varuna, Shiva and Brahma and many other gods came down in their celestial chariots that shone like the sun. They approached Rama who stood before them with his palms joined, eyes cast down respectfully, and said, 'How can you give Sita, who is so pure and chaste, to the fire? Do you not recognize her true nature?'

Rama replied in a soft voice that he considered himself only a mortal. Hearing this, Brahma explained to him that he was the incarnation of Vishnu, born on earth to slay Ravana, and Sita, his wife, was the incarnation of goddess Lakshmi. When Agni, the god of fire, heard Brahma's words, he rose up, holding Sita like a precious gem. Sita now shone like the morning sun, her hair dark and flowing, adorned with golden ornaments that had been purified by the fire. Agni placed her in Rama's lap and said to him in a forceful voice that echoed in all the three worlds, 'Here is your Sita, your beloved wife. There is no evil in her, neither in speech nor in mind, nor in thought, nor in glance. She is the most virtuous of all wives. She has never thought of anything else but you and prayed for your safety. She has suffered due to no fault of hers and even then her thoughts were never against anyone. When you left her alone in the deserted forest, and she was miserable and powerless, she was carried away by the rakshasa Ravana, who wanted to avenge an insult to his sister. She remained forever loyal to you. Though Sita was imprisoned and hidden away in a dark corner, her thoughts were always on you. She was guarded day and night by deformed, hideous rakshasa women. She was tempted and threatened, yet she never even looked at that evil Ravana, for she belonged with her entire being only to you. Accept her, for she is pure and chaste.' Agni declared this, his flames dancing around Sita and Rama.

Rama heard him in silence and then he spoke to all the assembled gods. 'It was necessary that Sita should enter the purifying fire in the presence of all the people of the world. She had lived long in the house of Ravana and if I had taken her back at once what would the people think of me? Would they not say that Rama, the son of Dasarath, is lustful and childish? I know well that Sita, daughter of noble King Janaka, has given her heart to no other, that she is devoted and has kept her thoughts always upon me, but in order to convince the people that she spoke the truth, I had to spurn her publicly.' Then, as the demons and the monkeys rejoiced, he took Sita's hand and led her to his chariot.

But Sita was not destined to live happily ever after. In Uttara Khand of *Ramayana*, which many believe was not Valmiki's creation, Sita is once again made to enter the fire to prove her innocence but this time she does not return to life. Unable to bear her endless sorrow, she asks the earth which gave her birth to open and receive her once more. And then Sita, the most chaste and pious wife, disappears forever into the lap of her mother.

Radha

Radha's name is inseparable from Krishna's in Hindu mythology, yet she is not found anywhere in the most important Purana dedicated to Lord Krishna—the Bhagavata Purana. There are a few lines about a gopi who was chosen amongst all the other gopis to accompany Krishna into the forest.

'Her heart swollen with vanity since now she considered herself the best of womankind, the gopi asked Sri Krishna to carry her. He agreed and asked her to climb onto his shoulders but as soon as she touched him he vanished into the air leaving her humiliated and repentant.' Later works consider this gopi to be Radha and gradually over the years many wonderful tales of love were woven around her and her beloved Krishna.

There are various versions given about the origin of Radha in the later Puranas. According to the Padma Purana she appeared as a bhumi-kanya, earth-girl, when King Vrishabhanu was preparing the ground for a yagna, but the Brahmavaivarta Purana, giving a lengthy account of Radha's birth, says that she was born in Gokula as the daughter of Kalavati and Vrishabhanu. The text also says that she was born from the left side of Krishna. In the Devi Bhagavata Purana Radha is considered one of the five forces which helped Lord Vishnu in the process of creation. Narayana makes an obeisance to Radha with these words in the Devi Bhagavata Purana:

'Salutation to thee the supreme goddess, who resides

at rasamandala, who lords over rasa and is dearer to
Krishna than his own life. Salutations to the mother of
all the three worlds, whose lotus-like feet are worshipped
by gods headed by Brahma and Vishnu. Be propitiated,
O Ocean of Mercy.'

Radha, like Sita, is seen primarily in relation to a
male consort though there are religious sects in Bengal
and Uttar Pradesh which worship her as an independent
goddess. Unlike Sita, Radha's relationship with Krishna
is not as a devoted wife. Instead, she gives herself up
totally to form an illicit relationship with her beloved.
Radha's love for Krishna is an obsession which makes
her break all norms of society and disregard her family
to be with her divine lover. Radha and Krishna's love
tales take place during Krishna's youth in the village of
cowherds in Vraja and in the romantic woods of
Vrindavan. Radha's love life is full of highs and lows as
she hovers between despair and ecstasy. Krishna loves
her with true passion, yet he cannot help sporting with
the other gopis just to torment her. She is his favourite,
but their love play is full of jealousy and longing.

In the *Gitagovinda*, a beautiful poem composed by
Jayadeva during the twelfth century, we see Radha as a
fully developed personality for the first time. The theme
of the poem is Radha's intense love and longing for
Krishna, her total devotion to him, regardless of anything
else. This powerful love relationship of Radha and

Krishna is seen as a metaphor for the divine–human relationship, with Radha representing the human devotee who gives up her entire being to be one with god.

In *Gitagovinda* Radha is seen as a lovelorn heroine, always pining for her lover. The dominant emotion of this great poetic work is viraha ras, or love in separation. In lyrical verse, the poet describes Radha's longing for Krishna, her jealousy and sorrow. She loves him with all her heart, defying society, against her own will even though he is not always faithful to her.

'My mind counts the multitude of his virtues, it does not think of his roaming even by mistake, and it possesses delight, it pardons him his transgressions from afar; even when fickle Krishna delights among the girls without me, yet again my perverse mind loves him! What am I to do?'

Radha is a married woman and in some Puranic texts older than Krishna. Her illicit love for Krishna and its power as a religious metaphor fascinated many poets in the thirteenth and fourteenth centuries. In their works, we see Radha as a tragic heroine torn between her overwhelming love for Krishna and her reputation as a respectable wife. She knows how dangerous it is for her to indulge in this secret loveplay. She has no formal claim on her beloved and can only meet him secretly in the darkness, hiding in the woods of Vrindavan. For every tryst with her lover she must risk the dangers of the night, the lonely woods and the disapproval of the village society.

> 'If I go to Krishna I lose my home
> If I stay I lose my love'

Radha's tormented love for Krishna inspired the fourteenth-century poet Chandidas to say:

> 'I who body and soul
> am at your beck and call,
> was a girl of noble family.
> I took no thought for what would be said of me,
> I abandoned everything.'

Radha's love for Krishna is praised by poets as the purest form of divine love. To this day, Krishna devotees consider Radha's love for Krishna as selfless love which expresses itself without any formal obligations on her part. She goes against the ways of the world to express her love and hopes to gain nothing. Radha loves Krishna in spite of everything just as a true devotee should.

Radha is considered by the poets as the ideal of feminine beauty which was described in the epics. She follows the same image as Sita and Draupadi and like them she too is slender, with limbs as delicate as spring blossoms. Her eyes, hands and feet are like lotuses and her breasts round and swelling, her thighs firm and hard, her lower lip like the sweet red bimba fruit, her hair dark and curly, her brows curved like serpents. The poet Jayadeva, who was an ardent Krishna devotee and faced many hardships because of his single-minded devotion, gives a beautiful and poignant description of Krishna's love for Radha.

'The pleasures of her touch and the tremulous, tender wandering of her eyes, the fragrance of the lotus which is her mouth, the cunning flow of the nectar of her words, the mead from her bimba-like lower lip—if thus, even in attachment to sense objects, my mind is fixed in the highest meditation upon her, alas, how then can the sickness of love-in-separation increase.'

In the *Gitagovinda* Radha is depicted as a passionate, proud woman who is often distraught despite being loved by Krishna since she cannot accept the fact that he belongs to the other gopis as well. Her anger makes her torment herself even when her beloved is with her. 'When the beloved Krishna is tender you Radha are rough, when he bends down in obeisance you are unbending, when he is passionate, you are hostile, when he has his face raised in expectation you have your face turned away . . . O perverse woman . . .'

The endless see-saw of Radha's love life, her emotional traumas of a love-sick heart, was seen as a metaphor for an unhappy devotee who could not find the lord even though she searches relentlessly to unite with him. In later texts, however, Radha's position is elevated and she is seen as Krishna's only beloved, his chosen lover. Exultant and flushed with joy she tells him in a poem by Surdas, 'You become Radha and I will become Madhava.' In another verse Krishna says to her,

> 'As you are, so am I; there is certainly no difference between us.
>
> As whiteness inheres in milk, as burning in fire, my fair lady,
>
> As smell in earth, so do I inhere in you always.'

In this story from the Brahmavaivarta Purana which considers Radha a goddess, we see her as Krishna's partner. But her life of trauma begins due to a curse.

Radha and Krishna lived and loved in a celestial city of incredible beauty called Goloka—the Cow-world—which was higher than Vaikunth, Vishnu's abode. This lovely place which was devoid of mental or bodily pain, disease, death, sorrow or fear was where silvery rivers flowed and woods were full of cooing doves and dancing peacocks. Here Radha danced like a queen with her beloved Krishna. She knew in her heart that she was the chosen one and belonged body and soul to the lord. The great Brahma himself had proclaimed to Radha, 'You are the outcome of the body of Krishna and equal to him in every respect. No one can say which of you is Radha or Krishna. He represents the soul of the world and you are its body and receptacle.' Time flowed endlessly here with no days and nights separating them as Sri Krishna, bedecked in a yellow dress as bright and pure as fire and ornaments of gold, his brow decorated with sandal paste, his neck adorned with wreaths of pearls, sported with Radha in an endlessly ecstatic dance. Radha, shining like a diamond necklace on Krishna's body, was the mistress of Rasa, and served her lord.

Everything was perfect in this never-ending blissful state as Radha and Krishna sported in Goloka. They danced their eternal dance watched by the other gods. Sometimes the pair hid in the emerald bowers like two doves and then again they emerged to dazzle everyone with their lustre. Hundreds of years went by thus and then one day the dark clouds began to gather. Radha held her breath and watched the darkening sky. She knew in her heart that her life of endless joy was about to be broken by someone. The days of bliss were now over and she could feel a new sense overwhelming her body. 'Is this called fear?' she asked herself.

Then came the day of sorrow which she had been

expecting. Sudama, a childhood friend of Krishna, angered by her sudden jealousy over another gopi, cursed her after a bitter quarrel. 'You will descend to the earth and be born a woman,' he said, anger blazing in his eyes. 'You will wander the earth as a common milkmaid. Thus you shall fall from your exalted position as a result of your jealous heart and this curse of mine.'

Radha heard these words and turned to Krishna, 'O destroyer of fear. How shall I bear this curse? How can I live without you even for a moment? You are my life, soul, vision and I am merely the body. My master, I cannot live without serving you. I shall surely die.' Lord Krishna, who knew what was to happen, consoled her. 'Fair one, in the Varaha age I shall descend to the earth. It has been predestined that you will go with me and be born on earth. Goddess, there I shall go and make merry with you in the forest of Vraja. Why should you fear, my beloved, when I am by your side?'

Thus Radha came to be born in Gokula as the daughter of Vrishabhanu. At the age of twelve she was married to Ayana, the brother of Krishna's foster mother, Yashoda.

An episode from the Brahmavaivarta Purana tells us that the marriage of Radha to Ayana was just a game of illusion. Radha's shadow was wedded to Ayana and she was actually Krishna's bride. The following legend describes their first encounter.

Krishna was born, as ordained, in the house of Nanda and Yashoda a few years after Radha had been born in Gokula. One day Nanda had taken his baby son to the forest to graze the cows. Suddenly, through the illusion and supernatural powers of baby Krishna, the sky became overcast and the forest assumed a fearful dark-blue light. Thunder crashed around them furiously and streaks of lightning struck the trees in the forest, making them sway dangerously. Nanda, distraught, ran about collecting his scattered herd and did not know how to manage the baby Krishna. Just then, by good fortune or by Krishna's desire, Radha happened to come by. 'Fear not. I will take care of your son,' she said. A swift dart of light fell on her from the sky as she took the child from Nanda and carried him to a bower of flowers. Radha's beautiful face began to glow as if her features were touched by a golden light. A fragrance of musk rose from her body and her mind was filled with a strange longing. As Radha clasped the baby Krishna to her breast she was reminded of her former life. With a thrill of rapture she remembered the sphere of rasa, the bed made of flowers inside a mansion built with gems. Then as she shut her eyes and recalled her past life, she was surprised to hear the sound of Krishna's laughter. She remembered that he had once been her divine lover. Aching with love, she opened her eyes and found a young boy by her side. His skin was dark blue, his eyes as beautiful as buds. His face seemed to have stolen the beauty of the full moon. Radha gazed at him in wonder.

They looked at each other in love and then Lord Krishna, smiling, said to Radha, 'My beloved, recollect the days of Goloka. I must fulfil the promise I made to you. You are dearer to me than my life. You are the container of the world and I am the cause. Therefore, O chaste one, come and occupy my heart. As an ornament bedecks the body, come and adorn me.'

Then Krishna lifted Radha's face to his and looked at her with love. 'Remember how we played under the flower-filled bowers; how we chased the moonbeams from our heads? I must fulfil the promise I made to you. You are dearer to me than my life. Let us dance the dance of eternal love once more.' As his honeyed voice filled Radha with ecstasy, suddenly Lord Brahma, the priest of the gods, appeared, wishing to perform a marriage ceremony for them. The sound of trumpets and drums came from the skies along with a shower of flowers as he married them and went back to heaven.

When Radha and Krishna were alone, she gently applied a paste of aloe and sandalwood, saffron and musk on his chest and Lord Krishna held Radha by the hand, embraced and kissed her and loosened the cloth which covered her body. All the cosmetics she had applied to make herself even more beautiful were wiped out by Krishna's embrace. The red hue of her lips was removed by his kisses, the chignon was unravelled, the lac-dye on her feet and the vermilion on her hair were smeared as Krishna made love to her. A small bell worn by Radha around her waist as an ornament was torn from her body by the passionate embraces of her lover. Radha lost her reason and could not distinguish day from night as thrills of rapture flooded her body. But then, later on, as she recovered her senses and looked up shyly at Krishna, he was no longer there. In an instant he had taken the form of the infant again and was now crying with hunger. He was exactly in the same place as Nanda had left him and Radha picked him gently in her arms. Tears flowed down her cheeks as she ran as swiftly as she could to Nanda's house. Yashoda was waiting outside the door looking up at the darkening sky with a worried face. She was overjoyed to see Radha with baby Krishna in her arms. 'Take him, he is hungry for milk. I must go home now, I have been away for so long,' said Radha and turned towards her home. But her heart was not sad any more because she knew that from now on she would see her beloved every day. Every day she would go to the sphere of rasa to dance the rasalila with Krishna. Had he not promised to her in another life: 'In the sphere of the rasa, you will sport with me . . . As I am, so you are . . . I constitute your life and you constitute my life . . .'

And so their eternal play continued and they lost themselves in the rapture of their dance, producing a flow of bliss for all the people of the earth who heard the call of Krishna's flute as it sang for Radha.

Radha's love for Krishna was a secret between them and she had to steal out at night to meet him. The poets were very taken by this adulterous, secret love and idealized it. Radha was called a parakiya, or another man's woman. If there is no parakiya there can be no birth of bhava. It is in fear of separation that grief and passionate longing grow.

Every night Radha goes out in secrecy and darkness wearing a dark cloak and silencing her ornaments. 'Abandon the noisy, capricious anklet, go to the dense dark grove; wear a dark blue cloak,' wrote Jayadeva. Radha is not afraid of the dark night, what she fears is not finding Krishna. 'I went to his hut in the secret thicket; secretly at night he remained hiding; I looked fearfully in all directions; he laughed with an abundance of passion for the pleasure-of-love.'

Every night Radha would wait for her husband and

mother-in-law to fall asleep and then creep out silently through the door like a thief. She was not afraid of the dark because it helped to hide her but she feared the villagers who might be awake at this late hour. She was also afraid of the evil spirits that lurked in the forest but she thought of Krishna waiting for her and ran towards the dark woods. She could hear his flute now playing faintly from behind a mango grove and the sweet sound made her faint with love. Then suddenly Krishna caught her in his arms, merging his blue skin with her milky white softness. They spent a magical night together, dancing the eternal dance of love as the gods watched from heaven. Then Radha, tired by his passionate lovemaking would lie in his arms, lulled to sleep by the sound of his flute.

Radha's absence from the house at night was noticed by her mother-in-law, Jatila, who had been watching her for some time. The dark shadows under her eyes, her langorous yawns made her suspect Radha had a secret lover. 'My son is never with her either at night or during the day yet she glows with love,' thought Jatila and decided to follow her one night. The moon rose early that night, reaching high above the forest from where it cast its silvery light over the paths. The trees gleamed like white arrows which had been struck by some warrior on the ground. 'O! Why do you shine tonight with such fervour? Have you too turned against my love? See how your light makes the path to the forest so clear and my way so dangerous. Can you not hide your bright face for a few moments behind a dark cloud so that I can run swiftly to my love?' said Radha. Then suddenly she heard footsteps behind her. She tried to run faster but a thorny bush caught her cloak and just then her mother-in-law appeared from behind a tree. 'O Radha, tell us where you are going at this late hour when the whole world is asleep. Tell us, girl, who awaits you in that dark forest where even brave men are afraid of venturing in full daylight? Speak the truth. We wait to hear your voice, your husband, these good women from our village and I,' cried Jatila angrily. Radha, wrenching her cloak free, began to run towards the forest. 'Wait, tell us where you are going,' shouted her husband trying to catch her hand. 'I am going to pray to the goddess Katayani,' said Radha. 'I do that every night. She stands beneath a bower beyond that hill. I take her fruits and flowers each night,' Radha's heart beat with fear.

'But you carry no fruits or flowers girl,' said a woman, peering at her through the trees. 'I will gather them now. I must go or the auspicious hour will pass,' said Radha as she ran ahead. Krishna was waiting for her near the bower, his blue form glowing like a precious gem. A fragrance of sweet champa blossoms floated in the air. Radha fell into his arms crying with fear. 'O my love, I have told such lies. I told them I was going to pray to Katayani. What shall I do now?'

Krishna caressed Radha's hair, soothing her trembling body with his gentle touch. 'Then you shall pray to Katayani, my beloved,' he said and laughed. With a flash of brilliant light which blazed right up to the sky, frightening all the creatures in the forest, shaking the earth violently, Krishna transformed himself into the goddess Katayani.

When Jatila, Ayana and the village women reached the bower beneath the hill, they saw Radha bowing before the goddess. Flowers of different colours and fresh fruits lay by her as she prayed with her eyes shut. A strange blue light surrounded Radha as if the goddess was blessing her. Ashamed that they had suspected her, everyone went away, leaving Radha alone with her divine lover.

Radha, unlike most goddesses, does not possess a gentle, placid nature. Her proud and passionate image is celebrated in popular legends, poetry as well as in miniature painting and dance. This legend speaks about her intense jealousy and pride which constantly torments her relationship with Krishna. This too is seen by Krishna's devotees as a token of extreme love and passion for the playful, cowherd god.

The day had passed full of sorrow and evening brought no respite. Radha searched every part of Vrindavan, every shade-giving tree, every bower full of flowers but she could not find Krishna anywhere. 'Where has he gone? Find him for me, dear friend, or I shall die of a broken heart,' she lamented to one of the gopis. Her hair, unadorned with flowers or jewels, streamed down like a turbulent river down her back, tears smeared the kohl in her eyes as she ran about like a mad woman, looking for Krishna. Finally a gopi took pity on her and told her the cruel truth. 'He has gone away with Chandravali—the gopi who has caught his eye with her flirtatious, bold manner. It is not his fault,' said the gopi, holding a trembling Radha in her arms. Radha's pain which pierced her heart like a poison-tipped arrow made her want to cry out but she was silent. She quietly returned to her house, keeping her face, racked with sorrow, hidden from passersby.

All through the night she wept silently, thinking about her beloved Krishna and Chandravali. She imagined him caressing Chandravali just the way he caressed and kissed her and her heart filled with anger. 'He touches her lips with the same soft touch as he did mine. O cruel love, do you remember me at all as you make love to her? Or has she erased all memory of our love from your heart?' she cried as the image of Krishna hovered above her, making her even more distraught. 'Will this night of sorrow never end? Will the moon never leave the sky? Do you linger on tonight, prolonging the hours of darkness because my love is making love to her?' she said, watching the moon through tearful eyes. Finally dawn touched the groves of Vrindavan and Radha went out to milk the cows. There, standing like a glowing flame of blue and gold, was Krishna. He smiled his heartbreaking smile, but Radha's anger now blazed out of her eyes as she beheld her beloved's face. His cheeks, which she loved to kiss, were besmeared with mascara from the other one's eyes. Vermilion streaks marked his chest and his lower lip was red and swollen with teeth-marks—a sign of the other one's passion. Radha's heart filled with anger and pain as she turned away, but Krishna's eyes, red from a sleepless night, would not leave her face. 'How he humiliates me by standing there, so openly showing the marks of his lovemaking on his body. Although he is guilty, he is not afraid; although he is threatened, he is not ashamed; although his crime is visible, he lies about it,' writes Jayadeva, describing Radha's anguish.

Radha finally controls her rage which was making her tremble and finds the strength to speak. 'You made me promises which you forgot when you saw her. You were to be with me and yet you spent the night with her. You are a pitiless, false lover. You make me burn with sorrow,' she said. Krishna tried to placate her with loving words and caresses but she would not stay and listen. Seething with anger and humiliation, she turned away from him and walked home.

Next day a sadhu came to beg at Radha's house. Her mother-in-law and some younger girls went to give him alms but he refused. 'I will only take food from the hands of a woman whose husband is alive. Otherwise I will go away empty-handed from this house,' he said in a loud voice.

Radha's mother-in-law, worried, quickly sent for Radha. 'Come, quickly. Bring some fruits and grain for this holy man. He should not go away from our house empty-handed.' Radha, weak and ill with an aching heart, refused to come out. Other members of the family grew agitated at her refusal and begged her again and again to come out. Radha finally stepped out reluctantly with some food but the holy man refused to take it. 'You must give me what I want,' he said. Radha, surprised, looked up at the holy man. She saw Krishna standing before her, resplendent in a saffron robe. None else could recognize him and her mother-in-law said to Radha, 'Yes, Radha, give him what he asks for. Then he will bless this house. Do not refuse him.' Radha, bewildered, did not know what to do. She could not refuse him since he was dressed like a holy man. 'What do you want from me?' she asked in a low voice. Krishna raised his eyes and looked at her with love. 'I want your pride.' Radha burst into tears as her love for Krishna overwhelmed her once more. Her aching heart was healed with the soothing touch of his loving glance as he took the offered fruits and left, promising to meet her in the bower at night.

Ganga

Ganga, rising from the snowy Himalayas and flowing down many miles into the Bay of Bengal, is considered to be one of the most important rivers of India. A subject of many myths, hymns, folk tales, popular songs and old sculpture panels, she is accorded the status of a goddess and is mentioned in many Puranas and in the *Ramayana* and the *Mahabharata*. Her divine origin endows her waters with the powers of cleansing all sins from the past, present and the future. During various auspicious days, thousands of people bathe in her waters in the holy cites like Hardwar, Rishikesh, Prayag and Varanasi. On her banks, the Kumbh Mela, considered to be the largest gathering of people in the world, is held where pilgrims offer prayers to the river. Most devout Hindus make the journey to the Ganga to scatter the ashes of relatives who have died, in the hope that the Ganga will absolve their sprits and make their journey to heaven easier.

The *Mahabharata* describes the virtues of Ganga with these words: 'If after death, the bones of the dead are deposited in Ganga the departed will attain heaven. Even if one has sinned throughout his life he would attain Vishnupada (heaven) if he worshipped Ganga. Bathing in the Ganga is as beneficial as performing a hundred yagnas. As long as the bones of one remains in the waters of the Ganga so long will he occupy an honourable seat in heaven. He who has come in contact with its water will shine forth as the sun, devoid of all darkness. Places which are not favoured by its waters will become barren like night without the moon and trees without flowers. Ganga water is more than enough to satisfy living things in all the three worlds.'

The Agni Purana too describes the greatness of the river: 'Through whatever places the Ganga flows those places become sublime and sacred. Ganga is the refuge of all created beings who aspire for the final good.' The heavenly Ganga is depicted in art as white in colour, and holding a lotus flower and a pot in her hands, she rests on a fish-like creature called the makaramatsya. Her image is often placed on temple doorways along with Jamuna.

In this tale from the *Ramayana* Ganga descends from heaven somewhat reluctantly.

There was once a mighty king of Ayodhya named Sagara who was childless. Anxious of having a son who would carry on his line, the king decided to do severe penance for a thousand years. At last, pleased with his worship, the saint Brighu granted him his wish. 'One of your queens will have one son who will carry on your name and the other shall have sixty thousand sons.' Soon the elder queen gave birth to a handsome son who was named Anshuman, while the younger queen produced a gourd. Just when she was praying to the gods in despair at not having had a single child, leave alone sixty thousand, the gourd burst into two parts. Out of its rind came sixty thousand babies who were carefully placed in jars of oil. They stayed in their dark retreats till they became young men. Then they rose up, all sixty thousand brothers, and stormed into the light like a vast army of warriors.

King Sagara, pleased with his good fortune, now planned a great yagna and Asvamedha which would not only extend his kingdom but take over the powers of even Lord Indra, the king of gods. Sagara sent Anshuman with a pure white horse into the neighbouring kingdoms. Wherever the horse went the countries became Sagara's because no king wanted to wage war with him. Soon Indra in heaven, worried as the horse began to get closer to his territory, decided to steal the horse and hide it in some safe place where none could find it.

Sagara was furious at this and sent his sixty thousand sons to search for the white horse. They looked everywhere but were not able to find it. Then they began to dig into the earth to reach the lower regions. But as they dug deeper and deeper, the gods began to get alarmed at their destructive work, fearing they would destroy the earth, and appealed to Brahma. The lord assured them that Vishnu would protect his bride, the earth, and halt the march of these sixty thousand sons of Sagara. So when they reached the core of the earth and found their horse standing near a sage who was meditating, the sons cried out in triumph. But before they could do anything, they were burnt to ashes by the sage Kapila who was actually Lord Vishnu in another form.

When Sagara could not find any trace of either his sacrificial horse or his sixty thousand sons, he sent his eldest son to look for them. Anshuman, after searching the entire world, finally reached the underground world where the ashes of his brothers lay scattered. Shocked and overwhelmed with grief, he broke down and began to cry. Just then Garuda appeared and consoled him with these words, 'Grieve not, O hero, for their death was ordained. The only way you can redeem their sins and set their spirits free is to get the holy river Ganga down to earth. It will not be an easy task and you must do severe penance for many hundred years to convince the gods to send their beloved Ganga down from heaven. But only her purifying waters can save your kinsmen from their terrible fate.'

The prince took the horse, but King Sagara was so disconsolate that, though he tried, he could not think of a way to bring Ganga down to earth. After his death, Anshuman too failed to liberate his brothers and finally this difficult task was left to his grandson, Bhagirath. In order to accomplish this, Bhagirath, who had no sons, decided to do severe penance for many thousand years in the hope that the gods would help him liberate his ancestors and also grant him a son and heir. Finally Brahma, pleased with his devotion, appeared before him and asked him what he desired. Bhagirath requested the god to send Ganga down to set his ancestors free and also asked for a son. Brahma agreed to grant him his wish but warned him that it may not be possible to hold Ganga when she descends. To solve this problem, the lord of creation gave Bhagirath this advice: 'I shall grant you your wish since you deserve it. I will order the heavenly Ganga to descend to the earth. But who will hold her torrent, which is like the force of a million charging horses? Ganga's waves will shatter the earth with the power of her current. Only a god can bear her force and not just any god but the lord of destruction. Shiva alone has the power to bear her descent. Try and win his favour if you can. Pray to him, O prince, since he is easily pleased and will surely grant you your wish.' Saying this Brahma returned to heaven, but Bhagirath remained standing in one place with his arms raised for an entire year till Shiva appeared before him and promised to hold Ganga when she descended to the earth.

Now Ganga was not at all pleased when she was told to go and flow on earth. 'No one asked me while all these plans were being made. Why should I go and liberate these sixty thousand humans? I am quite happy here in heaven and have no wish to descend to earth,' she said, tossing her beautiful head. But when Brahma commanded her she had no choice but to obey. As she prepared to descend, she hissed angrily to herself, 'With my flood I shall sweep him and whirl him into the deepest pool under the earth.'

Ganga made plans to fall from heaven with such fury that Shiva would never be able to contain her. That is how she would get her revenge, she thought, gathering her waves around her like a warrior preparing for battle. But Shiva, who knew what was happening in all three worlds, read her mind and laughed. 'Let her try whatever tricks she wants. I know how to subdue her,' he said. Then Ganga began to pour down from the heavens in such a rage that even the gods trembled. Her waters churning around like a whirlpool, her waves crashed out of the skies, ready to shatter the earth. As she got closer and was about to flood him with her torrent, Shiva looked up and smiled. Then he shut his three eyes and caught her in his hair. There he held her effortlessly like an eagle holds a sparrow. Ganga, surprised and even more angry now, twisted and turned, swirled around furiously but she could not set herself free, Shiva held her in the coils of his matted locks till gradually her anger abated. Then, made humble by Shiva's touch, Ganga flowed out as a gentle as a newborn calf. Her waves flowed into the sacred Vindu lake, from where she made her way into seven streams. One branch began to follow Bhagirath as he made his way to the place where his ancestors lay buried.

People of the earth rejoiced as they saw the heavenly Ganga following the king and came out to worship her with flowers and fruits.

But on the way Ganga made the mistake of flooding the sacrificial flame of a sage named Jahnu. In his anger, he drank up all the water and suddenly Bhagirath saw all his efforts coming to nothing. He again prayed to Brahma who came to his rescue, asking the sage to release Ganga. Jahnu agreed to do so but allowed Ganga to flow out of his ears. From then on one of Ganga's names became Jahnavi, or the daughter of Jahnu. Finally Bhagirath reached the ocean, and descended to the depths along with Ganga. They reached the place where the ashes of the sixty thousand sons of Sagara were lying and, as soon as Ganga touched them with her sparkling waters, the spirits of all the dead kinsmen of Bhagirath were set free. Purified by her waves, one by one they rose into the sky and made their way to heaven.

The *Mahabharata* unfolds its saga with King Shantanu falling in love with the heavenly maiden Ganga. This legend from the Adi Parva tells us how she became the wife of Shantanu and the mother of Bhishma—the grandsire and one of the most important heroes in the *Mahabharata*.

Once, while hunting on the banks of the river, King Shantanu saw a beautiful young woman. Mesmerized by her exquisite heavenly form, the king wanted to marry her at once. Forgetting everything, he offered her his love, his kingdom, his wealth and his life. Ganga was silent for a while and then when the infatuated king beseeched her over and over again, she agreed to be his wife. 'O noble king, I shall become your wife but only on certain conditions. You must never ask me who I am or where I have come from. You must never stand in the way of whatever I do, whether good or bad, right or wrong. You must never be angry with me on any account, however provoked you may be, or say anything that displeases me. Only if you agree to all these conditions, will I marry you but if you ever break any of these vows I shall leave you at once.' King Shantanu, deeply in love with her, agreed and they were married at once.

They lived a life of perfect happiness and bliss, unaware of the world around them. Then one day, much to Shantanu's joy, Ganga gave birth to a child. But his happiness turned to horror when Ganga took the newborn baby and cast him into the river. She returned home smiling gently, and King Shantanu, though distraught, could not break his promise to question her. Ganga had seven sons by Shantanu and each one she cast away in the river. King Shantanu's heart was filled with despair. 'Who is my beautiful wife? Where has she come from? Is she a witch or a heavenly form?' he wondered but dared not ask. 'Why did she drown her babies in the river?'

Shantanu watched his sons die one by one, and though he was crazed with grief, he did not break his promise to Ganga because he still loved her. He did not question her behaviour nor did he blame her for murdering his children. In silent anguish, he watched her take the newborn babies to the river and drown them. When she returned she always had a happy smile on her face as if she had accomplished something wonderful. Then after she had killed seven of his sons and was about to drown the eighth son, Shantanu's resolve broke. He followed her to the river and just when she was lifting the baby to throw him into the river, he stopped her. 'Pray do not drown this son of mine,' he cried, knowing he had broken his promise. Ganga turned to him in anger and said, 'O king, you have broken your word to me. You said you would not question anything I did however wrong it seemed. But love for your son made you forget your promise. Now I shall have to leave you but before I go let me tell you why I did these deeds which seemed wrong to you.' Then

Ganga began to narrate the story of the Astavasus to Shantanu.

One day, while roaming in the forest, one of the Astavasus, Dyau, saw the divine cow Nandini which belonged to sage Vasishtha. Dyau recalled that his wife had wanted this heavenly cow which gave milk all the time, so he asked his brothers to help him steal her. When the sage returned to his hermitage and found that Nandini was missing, he flew into a rage. With his divine powers he got to know at once that the Astavasus had stolen her, so he cursed them. 'All you eight Astavasus who have done this wicked deed will be born on earth as humans.' The Astavasus came rushing to Vasishtha and fell at his feet. 'Please forgive us, we have committed a great sin. O sage, we return Nandini to you. Please do not curse us to be born as humans just for our one mistake,' they cried. Sage Vasishtha's anger had subsided when he saw his beloved cow Nandini, so he changed the curse. 'You shall be born as humans but you will die and return to heaven at once. But you—Dyau—you were the one responsible for the theft. You will have to live on earth for a longer period.' As the Astavasus set out on their journey to the earth they met Ganga, who agreed to help them by becoming their mother on earth.

'That is why I had to drown our sons, who were the Astavasus, in the river one by one. This child who remains is Dyau. I shall bring him up and return him to you as my gift,' said Ganga and disappeared with the child.

Many years passed as King Shantanu ruled his kingdom in a wise and benevolent way. Then one day he was wandering along the banks of the Ganga when he saw a beautiful boy. To his amazement, the king saw that the little boy was amusing himself by casting a dam made of arrows across the raging river. The beautiful form of goddess Ganga suddenly appeared in the middle of the river and spoke to the king. 'This is Devavrata, the eighth son who I took with me. He has mastered every skill of archery, learnt the Vedas from Vasishtha. Take this son of ours, who will be a great hero.' Ganga gave the boy, who was covered with gold ornaments, to King Shantanu. Then she blessed them and went back to heaven. Devavrata later became the great hero Bhishma of the *Mahabharata*.

Village Goddesses and Minor Deities

Every village in India, however small or isolated, will have its own guardian devta or devi who looks after various aspects of the village. The village goddesses are considered especially important with far-reaching powers which affect even the most insignificant aspect of village life. Unlike the great goddesses, who are in charge of the celestial world and cosmic cycles, the main concern of the village goddesses is the village and its people. She is the presiding deity of the village, and her sole function is to guard the village people from the evil eye and keep its boundaries safe and secure from enemies. These local goddesses often do not have any anthropomorphic image and can be rough, uncarved stones or a tree. But they are worshipped with more affection and love than the greater goddesses since they belong heart and soul only to the village. The simple shrines dedicated to her are often built on the boundaries of the villages where the entire community gathers during festivals. Some local goddesses who have been established for a long time have their own temples where people from surrounding villages gather during important ceremonies. There is a friendly exchange of goddesses between certain villages in some parts of India where the younger goddess is taken, on certain auspicious days, with great fanfare to the temple of an older goddess. The villagers walk the entire length to accompany the goddess, with music and dancing. The worship of the local goddesses does not require the complex rituals which have been prescribed in sacred Hindu texts for other great goddesses like Durga and Lakshmi. A few grains of rice, a coconut or a goat, fruits and flowers will suffice for the local goddess who, if pleased, will protect the village from evil sprites, diseases and epidemics. She will ensure that the villager is blessed with good health, the women are fertile, the fields produce good crops and the rains come on time.

Besides villages, some cities like Kanyakumari, Kalka and Madurai are also associated with a particular goddess who is their guardian deity and has a temple dedicated to her in the city. While some of these goddesses are lesser known forms of goddesses like Durga and Lakshmi others are independent deities that exist only for the well-being and protection of that particular region. The origin of large cities like Mumbai and Kolkata are also traced back to a goddess who chose to reside in that place long before the city came into existence.

Unlike the popular legends about the great goddesses which are mentioned in the epics and the Puranas, the village goddesses live and act only in small, restricted areas, so the myths surrounding them too remain within the oral tradition of the village community, changing and evolving over the years to include local issues like festivals or natural disasters. The women narrate these legends so often during weddings, births and other ceremonies which fall on auspicious days that each child knows the stories by heart.

Kanyakumari is a temple town situated at the very southern end of India, dedicated to the virgin goddess. The story of her eternal love for Shiva is found in the Skanda Purana.

The great demon king Maya had a beautiful daughter named Punyakashi who worshipped Shiva. Her desire to merge with the god she loved with all her being was so great that she left her father's opulent palace, said to be the most wonderful in the three worlds, and went away to Kailash to meditate. After many hundred years of severe penance, Shiva appeared to Punyakashi and asked her what she wanted. 'I have loved you truly from the time I was born. I want to merge by being with you forever so that I may never be parted from you. I want to become not just your wife but a part of you,' said the young girl. Shiva agreed but told her to first go and meditate on the southernmost shore of the land, where she should wait for him till one second had passed. [Four lakhs and thirty-three years make one Yuga. The Kreta, Treta, Dvapara and Kali Yugas are the four Yugas. When two thousand such Yugas are over Brahma finishes a day. After a hundred years of Brahma are over the great deluge comes. Such ten deluges make a nazhika, or twenty-four minutes of Vishnu. Ten Vishnu deluges makes a second for Shiva.]

Punyakashi was happy to wait for Shiva on the southern shore where the three oceans met. Shiva also told her that she would have to destroy the demon king Bana who had grown very powerful. Since he knew he could only be killed by a virgin, he fought and destroyed all those who came in his way and even the gods were beginning to fear his strength.

As Punyakashi sat and meditated on the shore, Bana came there and fell in love with her at once. He was outraged when the young girl refused to marry him. 'How dare you, a chit of a girl, refuse the great asura who has conquered the three worlds?' he thundered and sent his two servants, the demons Darmukha and Durdarsana, to abduct Punyakashi. But the young girl, given immense strength by the gods, quickly slayed the two demons. Then she waited for Bana. A great battle took place on the shore which was watched by the gods. Finally Bana was killed by a lethal discus thrown at him by Punyakashi.

Now that her task of slaying Bana was over, Punyakashi waited eagerly for her beloved Shiva to arrive. But as the days passed, and Shiva did not come to her, her heart grew heavy with sadness. Now

Punyakashi realized that Shiva had never agreed to merge with her. He had only asked her to wait for him for an eternity. Gradually, in despair, she began to discard her jewels and bridal wear. The vermilion from her hair, the kohl from her eyes and the sandalwood from her skin merged into the sand and the sea to become a part of the seashore forever and the holy temple city that grew up at the spot was named Kanyakumari in her honour.

Manasadevi, the goddess of snakes, protects her devotees from snakebite. There are many legends about her great powers, many of them narrated by folk singers during festivals. In villages, offerings are made to her but she is given no image; instead she is worshipped in the form of an earthern pot and a snake made of clay. In some rare folk images she is shown as a woman dressed in a robe of snakes, sitting on a lotus or standing on a snake. The following legend is often sung during festivals dedicated to Manasadevi.

Once there was a rich and proud merchant named Chanda who refused to worship Manasadevi. Though his wife and other people of the village told him repeatedly to seek the goddess's blessing, he ignored them and expressed contempt for the Devi. Chanda had six sons who he loved dearly. He worked hard, gathering more and more wealth for them. One day his youngest son died of a snakebite. Chanda's wife, distraught and frightened, saw a bad omen in this unnatural death but Chanda did not pay any heed to her. Then his second son too died of a lethal snakebite when he was playing right outside their door. Now the entire village came out to warn Chanda, to make him believe in Manasadevi's powers but Chanda ordered them to go away. 'I do not care for this goddess of snakes and will never worship her,' he said. One by one all his sons died of snakebite till only the eldest was left. Chanda protected him day and night, never leaving him alone even for a minute.

The son was a handsome young man and he was soon married to a pretty girl from the village. To protect his son from snakes, Chanda had an iron house built for his son and his wife where nothing could enter, not even light. But Manasadevi still managed to send a snake through a crevice into the iron house and Chanda's eldest son too died on his wedding day. But the snake did not harm the bride who went weeping to her mother-in-law. 'Pray, ask your husband to repent. Ask him to beg the goddess's forgiveness. Then only will my husband return,' she cried. Now all Chanda's relatives and friends, village elders and priests came to his house and told him to change his behaviour towards the goddess.

Manasa herself appeared before his wife in a dream and asked her to reprimand her husband. Surrounded by a hostile crowd, the grief-stricken Chanda finally relented. 'What is there left for me to pray? She has taken all my precious sons. But I will do as you say.' Then he picked up a flower and carelessly threw it at Manasadevi's image. The goddess was pleased at this effort, however small and insignificant, and blessed Chanda with a shower of flowers. Then one by one she restored all his six sons to life. As everyone rejoiced, Chanda too realized the power and benevolence of Manasadevi and became her devotee from that day onwards.

The following legend from Uttar Pradesh is recited during fairs and festivals dedicated to the local gods of fertility. Professional storytellers gather a crowd of men, women and children by beating a drum and calling out the most interesting parts of the tale. Once enough people have responded to their call, they settle down under the shade of an old peepul tree and begin this tale.

There once lived a young girl who was very religious. Her family was very poor and the girl sold milk and curd to the neighbouring villages to make a living. Every day her mother-in-law would give her pots of milk and

curd to take to faraway places and when she returned
in the evening she would take the money from her. One
day after the rainy season had ended and the month of
Kartik had begun, she was passing a village when she
saw a group of women gathered around a peepul tree.
The girl, curious to see what they were doing, put her
pots of milk and curd down and went to the tree. She
saw that the women were watering the earth around
the peepul tree. 'Why are you doing this? It is an old
tree, it has no need for water,' she said. The women
replied that the tree goddess gave them her blessings if
they gave her water during the month of Kartik. 'She
will give us food, wealth and even return husbands who
have been lost for decades.'

The girl decided that she too would try to please
the tree goddess but instead of water she would give her
milk and curd. 'That way I will please her and gain her
favour.' So from that day onwards she began to pour
all the milk and curd her mother-in-law gave her around
the peepul tree. Every day the old woman asked for the
money she had got from selling the milk and curd, and
everyday she told her to wait till the month of Kartik
was over. Then finally when the month was over, on a
full moon night, the girl went and sat before the peepul
tree. That whole night she lay before the tree, till the
tree.goddess appeared and asked her, 'Why do you lie
here, girl? What do you want from me?' The girl folded

her hands with respect and replied, 'I have given all the milk and curd to you. Now my mother-in-law will ask me for money. What shall I do?' The tree goddess said, 'I have no money, child, but take these leaves and twigs and place them in a money box.' When the girl returned home her mother-in-law was waiting. 'Have you brought the money?' she asked angrily. 'Yes I have. It is in the money box,' said the girl. The mother-in-law opened the box and was amazed to see it overflowing with pearls, gold and jewels. 'Where did you get all this? Have you stolen it?' she asked, shaking the girl. 'No, the goddess who lives on the peepul tree gave it to me. I watered the earth around her roots with milk and curd every day. She gave me leaves and twigs in return to place in our money box and they turned into these jewels.'

The mother-in-law decided that she too would try and please the goddess. So from the next day she began to take the milk and curd to the village. But since she was a greedy woman, she sold the milk and curd first, then washed the empty pots and poured it around the tree. After a month was over she told her daughter-in-law to ask the goddess for money. 'How can I do that? It is not right for me to ask for money.' But the old woman ordered the girl to obey her, so she went to the tree and asked it to give her money. 'I have no money but take these leaves and twigs,' replied the tree. The old woman hurried back to her house and placed the twigs and leaves in her money box. 'Now you open the box,' she told her daughter-in-law. But when the money box was opened there were no jewels in it. Instead it was crawling with insects and worms. The old woman began to cry with horror, and then they heard a voice. 'The young girl gave milk and curd to me with a true love and devotion while the old woman did it just for greed. I have given them both what they deserved.'

From that day on women prayed to the peepul tree goddess by giving her milk and curd on the full moon night during the month of Kartik. As she pours the milk, each woman chants: 'Give us what you gave to the daughter-in-law and give none what you gave the mother-in-law.'

The goddess Shitala, the deity who is supposed to inflict as well as cure smallpox, is worshipped mainly in Bengal. She is represented as a golden-skinned woman dressed in a bright red saree and seated either on a lotus or a donkey. A pan of water is placed before her in the hope that she will ward off the dreaded disease of smallpox. Before the discovery of smallpox vaccine, the people of the villages used to take their children to the temple during an auspicious day and the temple priest would invoke the name of Shitala mata and make a kind of inoculation on the child's arm. Then water and flowers which had been blessed by the goddess would be given to the child to protect him from smallpox. If the disease did not attack the child then the parents would return with gifts for the goddess.

The following folk tale is recited during the auspicious day of Shitala shashti in spring when women fast and abstain from bathing in hot water or even cooking food.

There lived a wealthy old man who had seven sons. But though they had been married for many years none of the sons had any children. An elderly woman in the village advised the daughters-in-law to fast and pray to the Goddess Shitala who would bless them with sons. The seven wives did as they were told and were soon gifted with sons by the goddess who was pleased by their devotion. But later on, as the years went by, the old man's wife become careless and once during the fast, she decided to bathe in hot water. 'How cold it is today. You too bathe in hot water, what harm will it do,' she said to her daughters-in-law. They all obeyed her and happily began bathing in hot water.

That night the old woman woke up screaming. She had had a terrible nightmare in which her husband and all her seven sons were lying dead. She saw that their wives too were beginning to die one by one. The old woman began to rant and rave like a mad person when she opened her eyes and saw that her husband had actually died. Then when she saw herself being killed by an axe which she herself held in her hands she screamed. As her shrieks became louder and louder, the neighbours rushed to see what was happening and saw her thrashing on the ground, her clothes torn and her face swollen with fear and grief. They told her that she herself was to blame for this trauma. 'You broke the rules of the Shitala fast and bathed in hot water. This is what happens when you annoy the goddess,' they shouted.

The old lady, unable to bear her anguish, ran out of the house and kept running till she reached the woods beyond the village. Her head and hands seemed to be burning with fever and she stopped to rest in the shade of a tree. As she was rubbing her body with leaves to cool the burning of her skin, she suddenly saw an old woman burning like herself. Waves of heat were pouring out of her head, her skin was yellow and her eyes were red as if on fire. 'Kind lady, please bring me some cool curd to soothe this burning which is causing me so much pain.' When the old lady heard the woman speak, she realized at once that this was none other that the Goddess Shitala herself. 'I have caused her so much pain, I must do something at once to relieve her of this sorrow,' said the old lady and ran back at once to her village. There she gathered as much curd as she could in a pot and headed back to the woods. The people of the village tried to follow her but she vanished from the path as if she had never been there. The old lady found the goddess in the same place under the tree and after bowing before her, she began to smear her arms with the curd. Gently, with great love, she smeared the goddess's entire body with the curd till the burning of her skin had subsided. Then when the goddess sat peacefully with her eyes shut, the old woman fell at her feet and asked for her forgiveness. The goddess smiled and placed her cool hand over her head. 'Your husband will be alive again. You did no wrong. Go and pray with a true heart and I will take care of your family,' said Shitala and vanished. From then on the people of the village kept the fast of Shitala every spring for the well-being of their family.

Hymn to Aparajita

'Salutation to the Devi, to the Mahadevi. Salutation always to her who is ever auspicious. Salutation to her who is the primordial cause and the sustaining power. With attention, we have made obeisance to her.

'Salutation to her who is terrible, to her who is eternal. Salutation to Gauri, the supporter (of the universe). Salutation always to her who is of the form of the moon and moonlight and happiness itself.

'We bow to her who is welfare; we make salutations to her who is prosperity and success. Salutation to the consort of Shiva who is herself the good fortune as well as misfortune of kings.

'Salutation always to Durga who takes one across in difficulties, who is essence, who is the author of everything; who is knowledge of discrimination; and who is blue-black as also smoke-like in complexion.

'We prostrate before her who is at once most gentle and most terrible; we salute her again and again. Salutation to her who is the support of the world. Salutation to the

Devi who is of the form of volition.

'Salutations again and again to the Devi who in all beings is called Vishnumaya.

'Salutations again and again to the Devi who abides in all beings as consciousness;

'To the Devi who abides in all beings in the form of intelligence;

'To the Devi who abides in all beings in the form of sleep;

'To the Devi who abides in all beings in the form of hunger;

'To the Devi who abides in all beings in the form of reflection;

'To the Devi who abides in all beings in the form of power;

'To the Devi who abides in all beings in the form of thirst;

'To the Devi who abides in all beings in the form of forgiveness;

'To the Devi who abides in all beings in the form of genus;

'To the Devi who abides in all beings in the form of modesty;

'To the Devi who abides in all beings in the form of peace;

'To the Devi who abides in all beings in the form of faith;

'To the Devi who abides in all beings in the form of loveliness;

'To the Devi who abides in all beings in the form of fortune;

'To the Devi who abides in all beings in the form of activity;

'To the Devi who abides in all beings in the form of memory;

'To the Devi who abides in all beings in the form of compassion;

'To the Devi who abides in all beings in the form of contentment;

'To the Devi who abides in all beings in the form of mother;

'To the Devi who abides in all beings in the form of error; (Truth and error are both obverse and reverse forms of the Goddess.)

'To the all-pervading Devi who constantly presides over the senses of all beings and (governs) all the elements;

'Salutations again and again to her who, pervading this entire world, abides in the form of consciousness.

'Invoked of yore by the devas for the sake of their desired object, and adored by the lord of the devas every day, may she, the Isvari, the source of all good, accomplish for us all auspicious things and put an end to our calamities!

'And who is now again, reverenced by us, devas, tormented by arrogant asuras and who, called to mind by us obeisant with devotion, destroys this very moment all our calamities.'

(*Devimahatmyam*, 8-82, translated by
Swami Jagadiswarananda)

Bibliography

Bhagawata Purana; Gita Press
Devi Katha; Ramakrishna Mission
Devi Mahatmya; Chinmaya Mission, Madras
Devimahatmyam; translated by Swami Jagadiswarananda; Ramakrishna Math, Madras
Dhasha Devi; Randhir Prakashan
Folk Tales from Bengal; L.B. Dey; Subarnarekha
Gitagovinda; Jayadeva
Hindu Goddesses; D. Kinsley; Motilal Banarasidass
Hindu Myths; Penguin Classics
Mahabharata; translated by C. Rajagopalachari; Bharatiya Vidya Bhavan
Puranic Encyclopaedia; Motilal Banarasidass
Ramayana; T.H. Griffith; Luzac and Co.
Ramayana; translated by C. Rajagopalachari; Bharatiya Vidya Bhavan
Rig Veda; Penguin Classics
Sankshep Purana; Gita Press
Shiv Purana; Amit Prakashan
Srimatdevibhagwat; Gita Press
Tulsidas Ram Charit Manas; Gita Press